Mary

with happy memories of St. [illegible]

Love

[illegible]

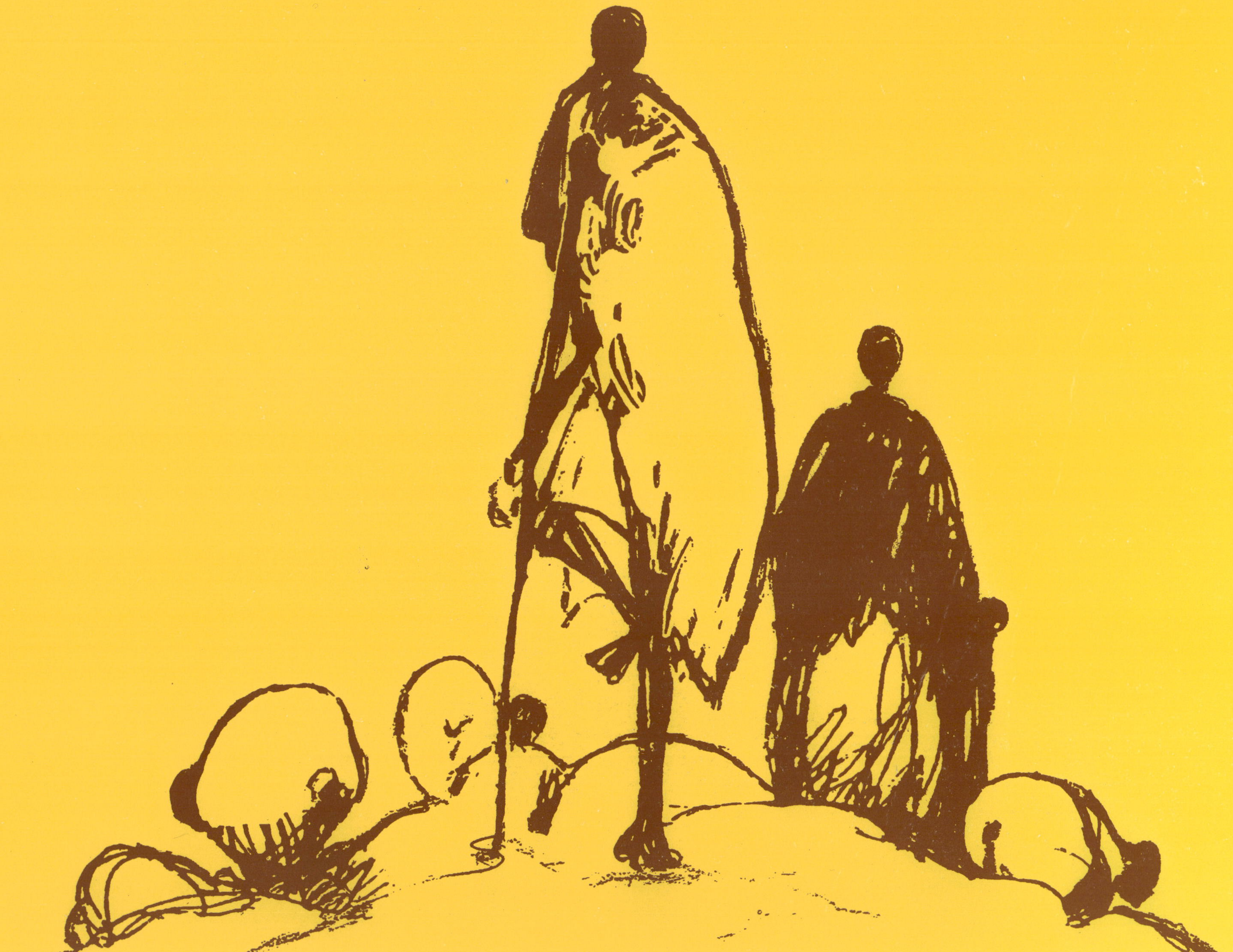

TONY HUDSON'S

Images Of Africa

By Dylan Hudson

This book is dedicated in loving memory to my father Tony Hudson.

With special thanks to:
My mother Barbara Hudson
Louise Hillier
Bridget King
Al Jackson of Masai Mara
All of my family and my girlfriend Nikki, for the help and support given to me while producing this book.

FIRST EDITION
Published by:
African Connection, 33 Fore Street, St Ives, Cornwall, England TR26 7RT.
Tel & Fax: +44 (0) 1736 793147.
ISBN 0 9533272 0 5

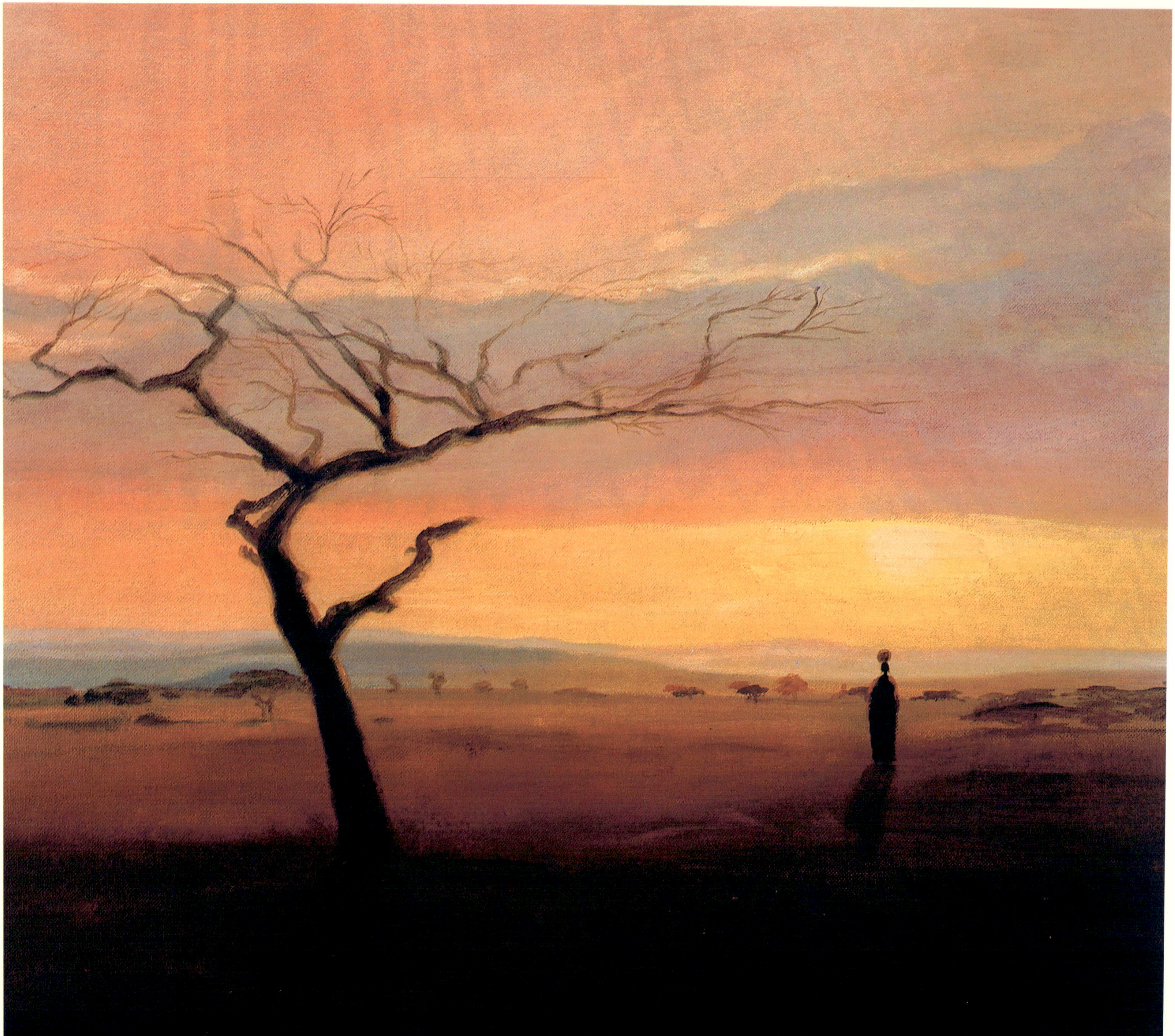

The cover picture: ***African Sunset*** *- Like this dramatic silhouette of a tree, the spirits of their ancestors overshadow the lives of the people in Africa. It is always best to be home before the sun sets, for the light of the fire keeps bad spirits at bay. (Acrylic)*

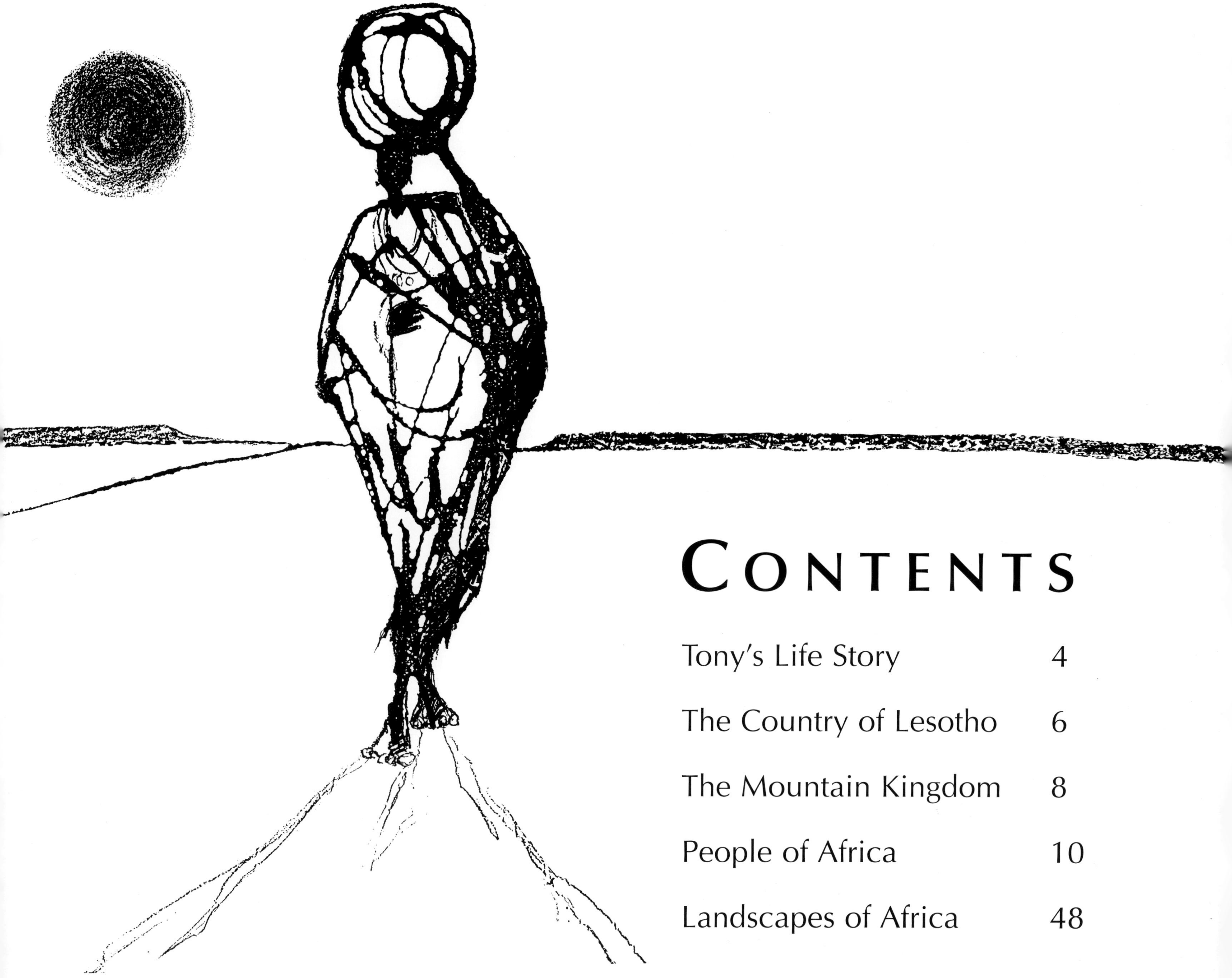

Contents

Tony's Life Story 4

The Country of Lesotho 6

The Mountain Kingdom 8

People of Africa 10

Landscapes of Africa 48

Tony Hudson

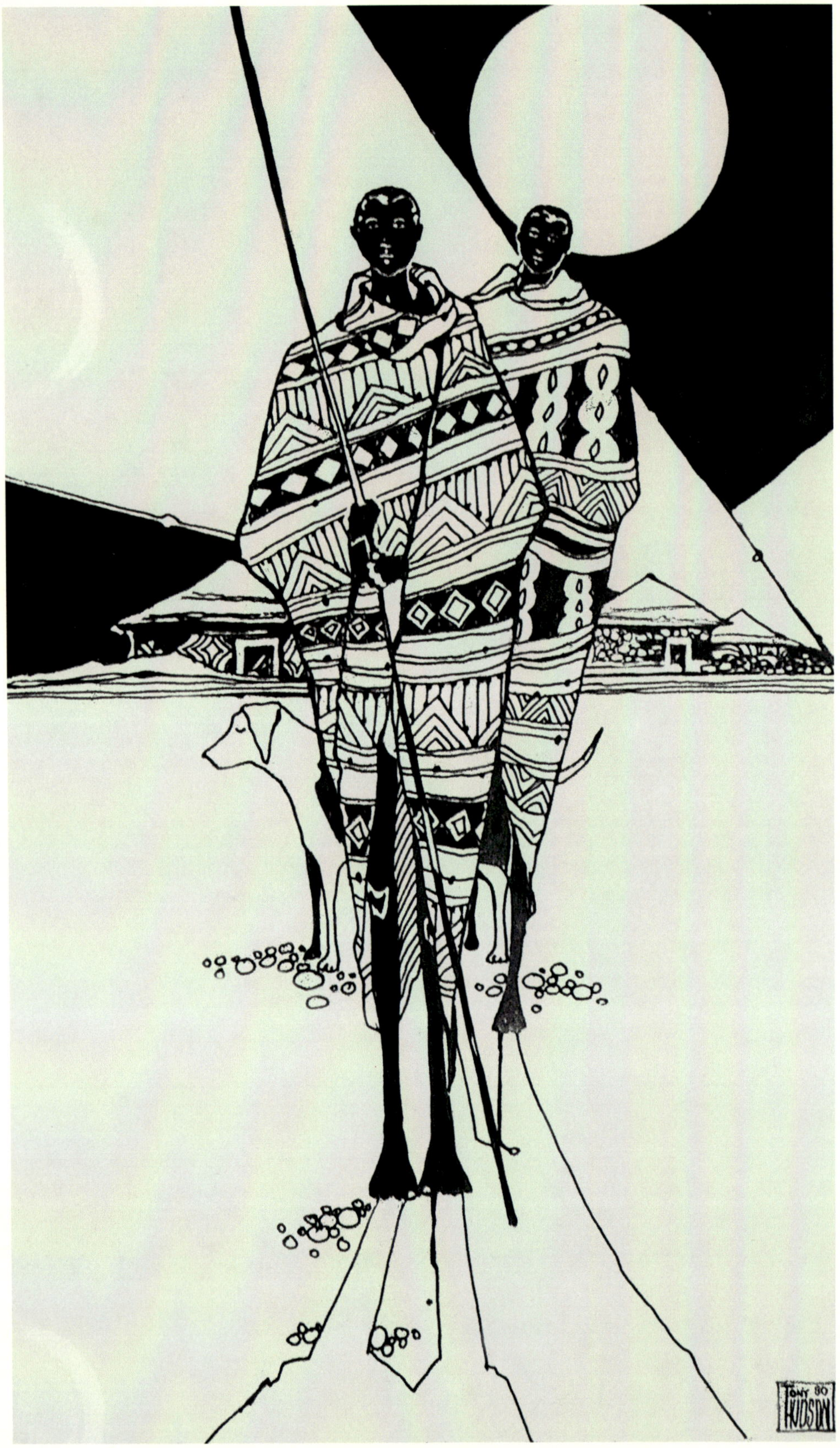

Above: ***By Design*** - *Strong lines and intricate designs represent the long and ancient tradition of the Basotho people as nomadic guardians of their livestock. (Ink)*
Opposite page: ***Blanket Design*** - *As elegant as any model, the Basotho women wear their blankets with grace and style as they protect themselves against the cold mountain air. (Ink)*

Tony was born in 1938 in Cradley Heath in the West Midlands of England. Christened Anthony Jack Hudson, Tony grew up wanting to be an artist, although his father wished him to become an auctioneer.

Tony was naturally talented and never attended art school but obtained a job in the art department of Cadbury's at Bourneville in Birmingham. Here he remembered working with his friend Dick Ferniheugh on a huge mural of the coco bean which may still hang in Cadbury House.

After leaving Cadbury's he worked for a design studio in Birmingham, working on a variety of projects, fashion drawings for magazines and many graphic art designs for catalogues, advertising, and publications.

In 1961 he married Barbara Jones and together with their son Mark moved from Birmingham to Quarry Bank in the West Midlands. In the spring of 1968 the couple moved to the village of Veryan in Cornwall where the vicar had built five round houses as a result of his visit to Lesotho. Tony worked on illustrating comic love stories, the text being sent all the way from Thompsons in Dundee. His drawings were much appreciated and Tony was the only artist to receive fan mail from avid readers around the country. During the weekends, Tony painted Cornish landscapes and seascapes. These, and the stoneware pottery which Barbara taught herself to make, they sold in their own art gallery which they had converted from a garage. In 1978 they moved to Falmouth.

A potter friend, Peter Hayes, had moved to Maseru, the capital city of Lesotho, where he was working at Thaba Bosiu Ceramics in the capital, Maseru. While on holiday in England, Pete spent a holiday with Tony and Barbara in Falmouth. He was looking for a potter to take over Thaba Bosiu ceramics, as he had been offered another position in the Lesotho National Development Corporation. Barbara jumped at the opportunity, and in 1979 the couple and their nine year old twins, Dylan and Kate, moved out to Lesotho in southern Africa.

While Barbara was busy building up the pottery, Tony found himself with time on his hands. He toured around Lesotho with an English water engineer and everywhere he went he filled his sketch books with images of the people, the horseman, the herdboys and the landscapes that inspired him. When he returned to his studio after a trip, he battled to refine the images he had captured. Because of his work as a commercial artist, Tony was able to use a wide variety of media to express himself. However, to find the right medium to capture the images he had in mind, took him considerable time and effort. After several months of hard work he was satisfied, and a flood of paintings began to emerge. After a year in Lesotho, the family moved back to live in England, firstly in Bath and later in St Ives, but Tony continued to explore the different themes he had developed in Africa and made regular return visits.

In all his paintings, whether inspired by Lesotho, the Transkei or other parts of Southern Africa, Tony's love of the people and the land shows through. His sensitivity and choice of colour, his range of technical skill in expressing the raw emotions of the continent, and his empathy with dramatic landscapes and open skies shine through in every work. Extremes of colds and heat; stillness and movement; youth and age are explored and exploited in his vibrant canvases.

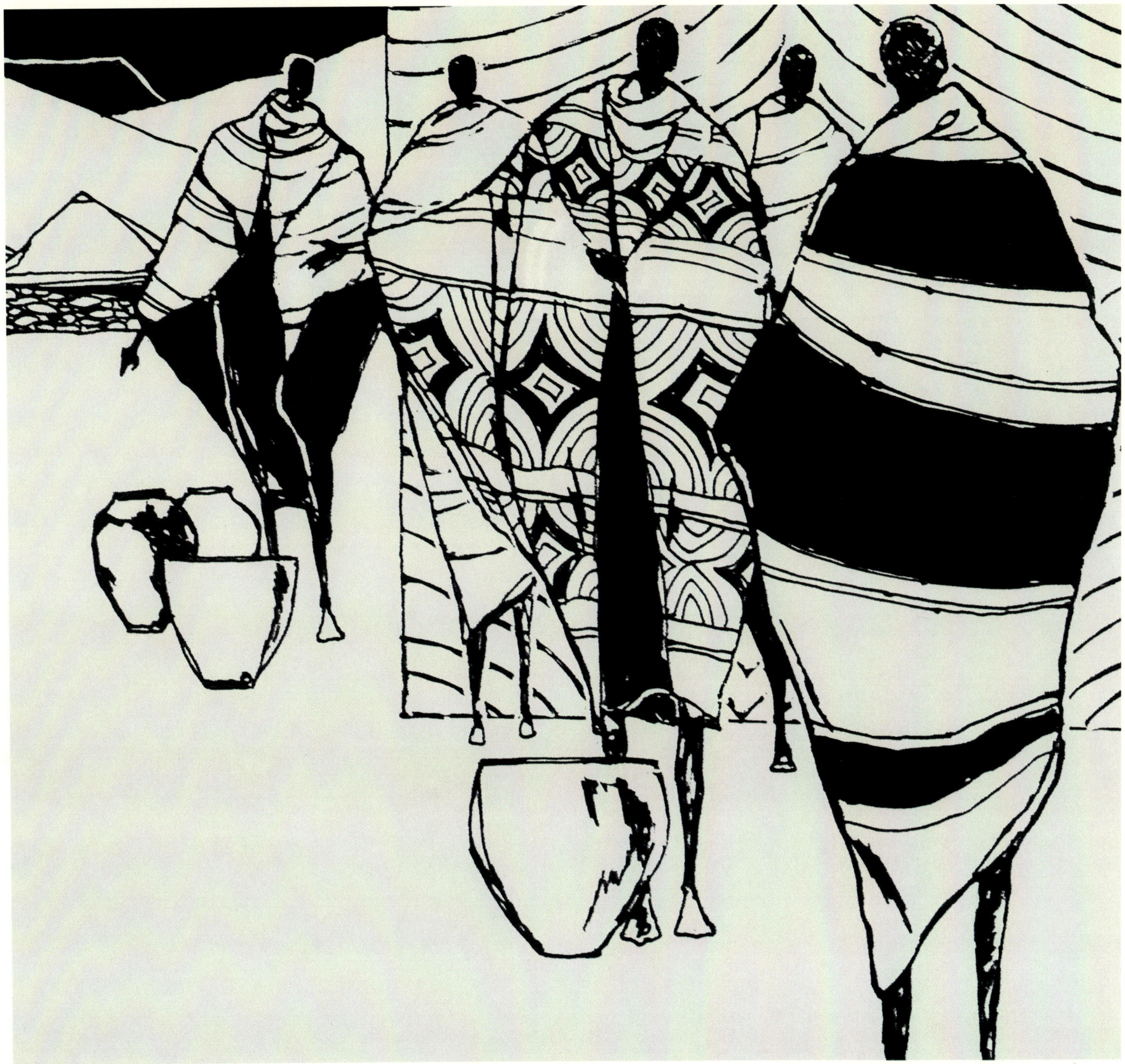

Between 1980 and 1989, Tony held many successful exhibitions of his paintings and drawings in Maseru and the queue of eager buyers grew each time. In 1989 the Queen of Lesotho attended a private preview of his exhibition at the Lesotho Sun Hotel, and the exhibition itself was a sell out. To celebrate this tremendous success, Tony, Barbara and their daughter Kate set off with a friend, Dawnia on a trip to the Kruger National Park in South Africa. The night before entering the park, they stayed in the town of Nelspruit and ate a good dinner before retiring to bed. During the night, Tony suffered a massive heart attack and died.

News of Tony's death spread throughout Lesotho immediately, causing immense shock and sadness to all who had known and loved him. It was arranged that he should be buried at the foot of Thaba Bosiu, the 'Mountain of Night', This impressive flat-topped rocky mountain was the strong hold from which King Moshoeshoe 1st had withstood the onslaught of the Boers and it was from here that the King begged Queen Victoria to extend her protection to the new Basotho kingdom.

At Tony's funeral the church was full with friends who had known him, bought his paintings, enjoyed his company and mourned with his family. Every possible space was filled by members of the village of Thaba Bosiu who were enormously honoured that such a celebrity should be buried in their midst. Tony's grave lies close to the parish church in which hangs his pencil sketch of King Moshoeshoe 1st, which was donated by Tony's widow. Visitors to Thaba Bosiu can obtain directions to the grave from the visitors centre at the entrance to the village.

Throughout his later life, Tony took colour slides of his paintings before they were sold to buyers from every corner of the world. These slides have been used to reproduce his work in cards and prints and have proved to be a tremendous source of financial support for the family he left behind. Barbara and her sons Dylan and Mark now run 'African Connection' a gallery in St Ives, Cornwall. From which they keep his name alive by selling the prints and other quality crafts from all parts of Africa.

Memories Accounted by Barbara Hudson (Tony's widow).

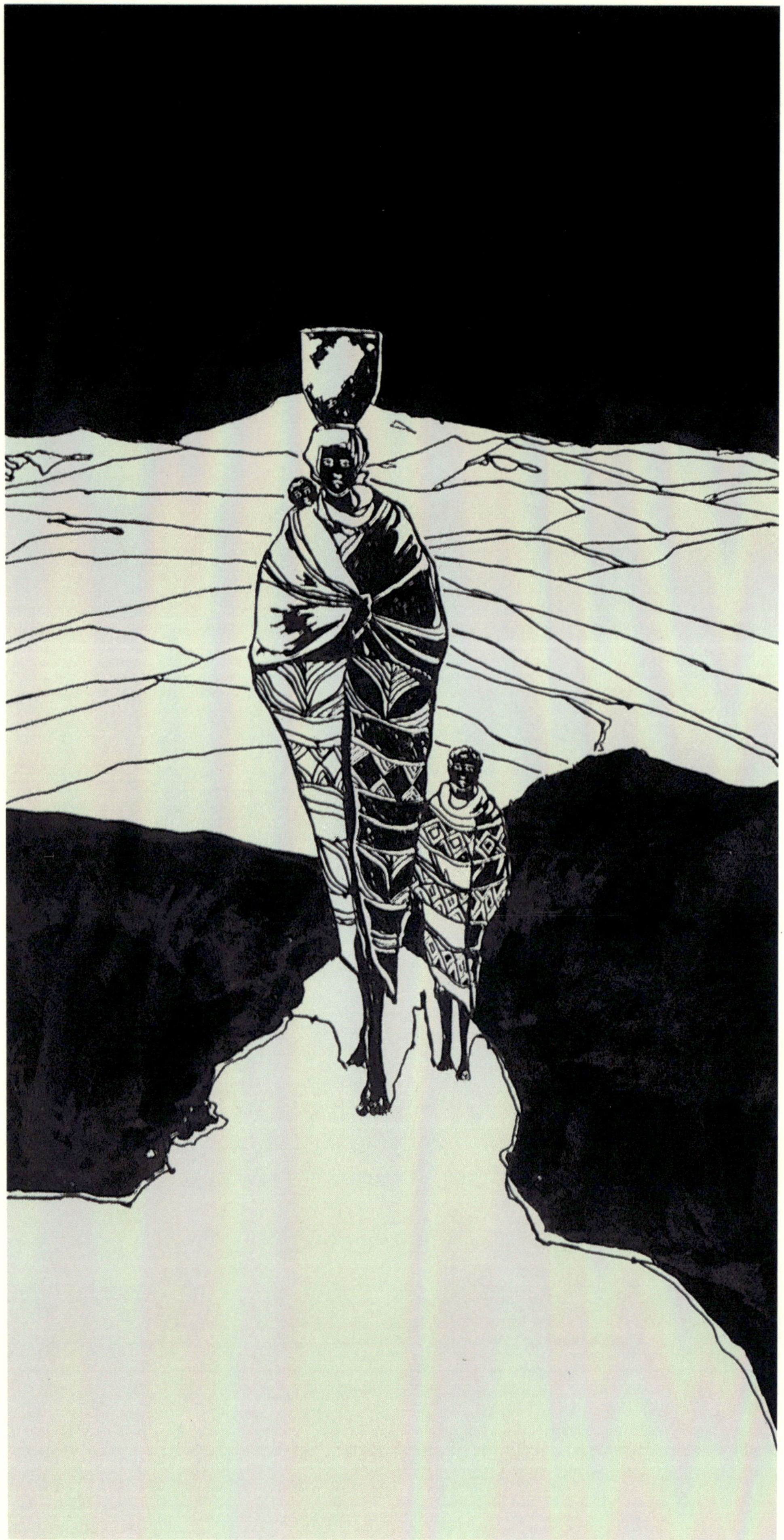

Lesotho

Land-locked Lesotho is a mountainous country and the only country in the world with all its land over 1000 meters above sea level. The western edge of the country is known as the Lowlands, but these, in fact, are very high plains, low only in comparison with the Maluti mountains that occupy nearly three quarters of the country.

The Maluti are formed from horizontal layers of rock broken by valleys and gorges eroded over millions of years. The various strata are clearly exposed, giving the mountains their extraordinary colours. There are layers of red, purple, grey and white with oranges and pinks, and depending on the time of day, other colours impose themselves.

Lesotho lies completely outside of the tropics and this, together with it's height above sea level, gives it a temperate and healthy climate.

The Pillar *- Tall and graceful, the woman emerges from the immense landscape and open spaces of Africa. Holding the future of the continent in her arms, she firmly guides her children into the future.*
(Ink)

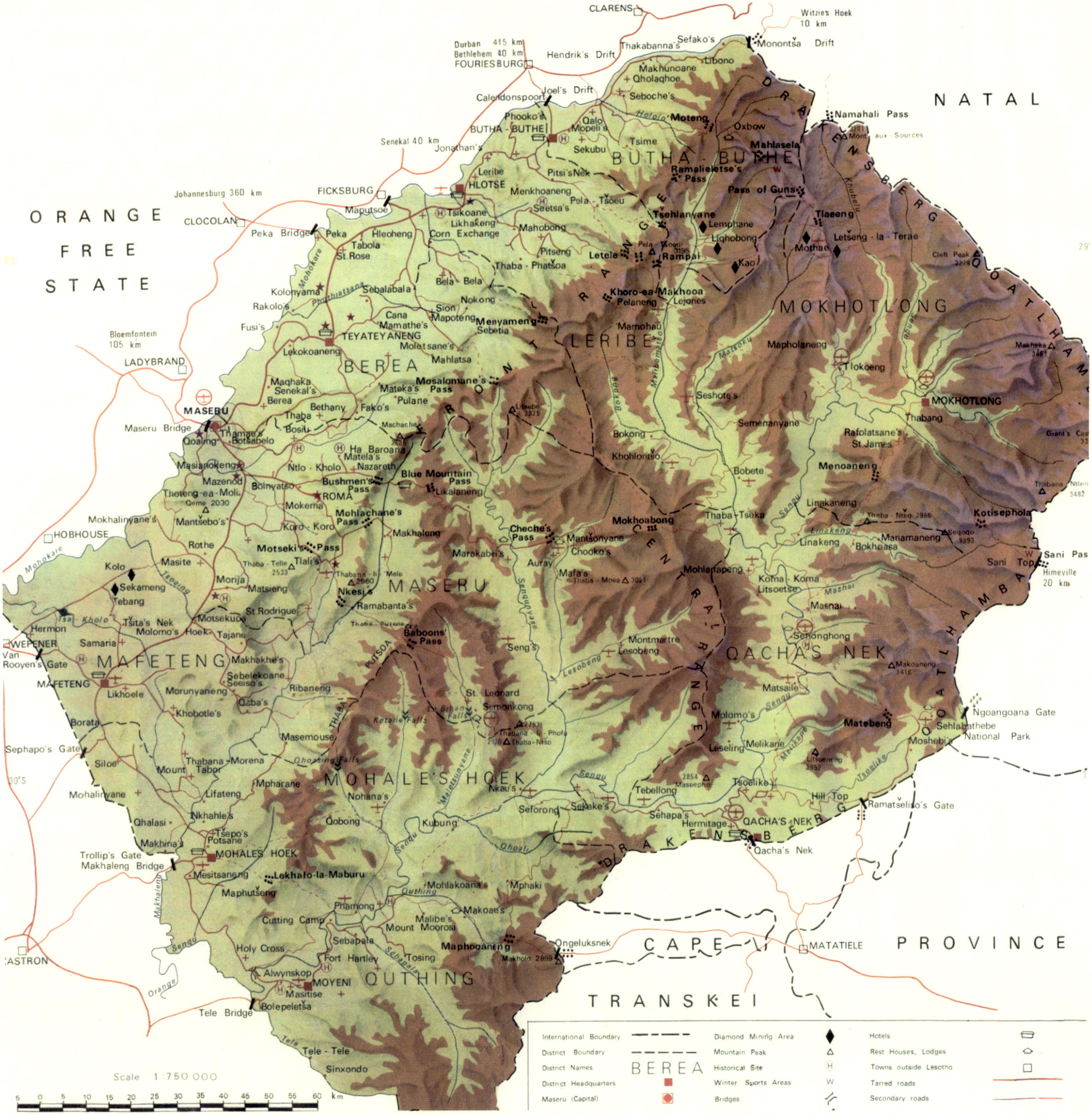

CLARENS
Witzies Hoek
10 km
Monontša Drift
Durban 415 km
Bethlehem 40 km
FOURIESBURG
Hendrik's Drift
Thakabanna's
Sefako's
Libono
Makhunoane
Qholaqhoe
Seboche's
NATAL
Calendonspoort
Joel's Drift
Phooko's
BUTHA - BUTHE
Qalo
Mopeli's
Moteng
Oxbow
Namahali Pass
Senekal 40 km
Jonathan's
Sekubu
Tsime
Mahlasela
BUTHA - BUTHE
Leribe
HLOTSE
Pitsi's Nek
Ramalieletse's Pass
Pass of Guns
Johannesburg 360 km
FICKSBURG
Menkhoaneng
Pela - Tsoeu
Seetsa's
Maputsoe
ORANGE
FREE
STATE
CLOCOLAN
Tsikoane
Likhakeng
Tsehlanyane
Lemphane
Tlaeeng
Peka Bridge
Peka
Hleoheng
Corn Exchange
Mahobong
Liqhobong
Mothae
Letšeng - la - Terae
Tabola
St.Rose
Pitseng
Letele
Rampai
Kao
Cleft Peak
Thaba - Phatsoa
Bela - Bela
Kolonyama
Sebalabala
Khoro-ea-Makhoa
Pelaneng
Lejones
MOKHOTLONG
Rakolo's
Nokong
Sion
Mapoteng
Menyameng
Sebetia
Cana
Mamathe's
Fusi's
TEYATEYANENG
Mamohau
Bloemfontein
105 km
Molet sane's
LERIBE
Mapholaneng
Lekokoaneng
BEREA
Mahlatsa
LADYBRAND
Tlokoeng
Maqhaka
Senekal's
Berea
Mosalomane's Pass
Mateka's Pass
Pulane
MOKHOTLONG
Seshote's
Bethany
Fako's
Thabang
MASERU
Thaba
Bosiu
Machache
Maseru Bridge
Thamae's
Botšabelo
Semenanyane
Rafolatsane's
St.James
Qoaling
Ha Baroana
Matela's
Nazareth
Bokong
Masianokeng
Ntlo - Kholo
Khohlontšo
Mazenod
Blue Mountain Pass
Menoaneng
Bobete
Boinyatso
Bushmen's Pass
Likalaneng
Thoteng-ea-Moli.
Qeme 2030
ROMA
Thabana Ntlenyana 3482
Mokhalinyane's
Mokema
Mohlachane's Pass
Linakaneng
Mantšebo's
Koro - Koro
Mokhoabong
Thaba - Tsoka
Kotisephola
HOBHOUSE
Makhaleng
Cheche's Pass
Mantšonyane
Linakeng
Bokhoasa
Manamaneng
Rothe
Motseki's Pass
Chooko's
Sani Top
Sani Pass
Masite
Thaba - Telle 2533
Tlali's
Marakabei's
Auray
Himeville
20 km
Kolo
Sekameng
Morija
Thabana - li - Mele 2660
Mafa's
Thaba - Moea 3041
Mohlanapeng
Koma - Koma
Litsoetse
Tebang
Matsieng
Nkesi's
MASERU
Masnai
Hermon
Tsita's Nek
Molomo's Hoek
Motsekuoa
St Rodrigue
Ramabanta's
Baboons' Pass
WEPENER
Samaria
Tajane
Sehonghong
Van Rooyen's Gate
MAFETENG
Makhakhe's
Seng's
Montmartre
Lesobeng
QACHA'S NEK
Makoaneng 3416
MAFETENG
Sebelekoane
Seeiso's
Ribaneng
Likhoele
Morunyaneng
Qaba's
St. Leonard
Semonkong
Matsaile
Ngoangoana Gate
Khobotle's
Borata
Katane Falls
Molomo's
Matebeng
Sehlabathebe
National Park
Masemouse
Thabana - li - Phofa
Thaba - Ntso
Sephapo's Gate
Siloe
Thabana - Morena
Leseling
Melikane
Moshebi's
Mount Tabor
Qhoali Falls
30°S
Mohalinyane
MOHALE'S HOEK
Mpharane
Nkau's
Tebellong
Tsoelike
Lifateng
Nohana's
Maseepho
Litsoeneng
Hill Top
Ramatšeliso's Gate
Qhalasi
Nkhahle's
Qobong
Seforong
Sekake's
Sehapa's
Hermitage
QACHA'S NEK
Makhina's
Tsepo's
Potsane
Kubung
DRAKENSBERG
Qacha's Nek
Trollip's Gate
Makhaleng Bridge
MOHALES HOEK
Mesitsaneng
Lekhalo-la-Maburu
Maphutseng
Mohlakoana's
Mphaki
Phamong
Makoae's
Cutting Camp
Malibe's
Mount Moorosi
Sebapala
Maphooaneng
Ongeluksnek
CAPE
PROVINCE
MATATIELE
Holy Cross
Fort Hartley
Tosing
Makholo 2889
ZASTRON
Alwynskop
MOYENI
QUTHING
Masitise
TRANSKEI
Tele Bridge
Bolepeletsa
Tele - Tele
Sinxondo
DRAKENSBERG
MALOTI RANGE
FRONT RANGE
CENTRAL RANGE
QUATHLAMBA
Scale 1:750 000
5 0 5 10 15 20 25 30 35 40 45 50 55 60 km
International Boundary
District Boundary
District Names
BEREA
District Headquarters
Maseru (Capital)
Diamond Mining Area
Mountain Peak
Historical Site
Winter Sports Areas
Bridges
Hotels
Rest Houses, Lodges
Towns outside Lesotho
Tarred roads
Secondary roads

The Mountain Kingdom

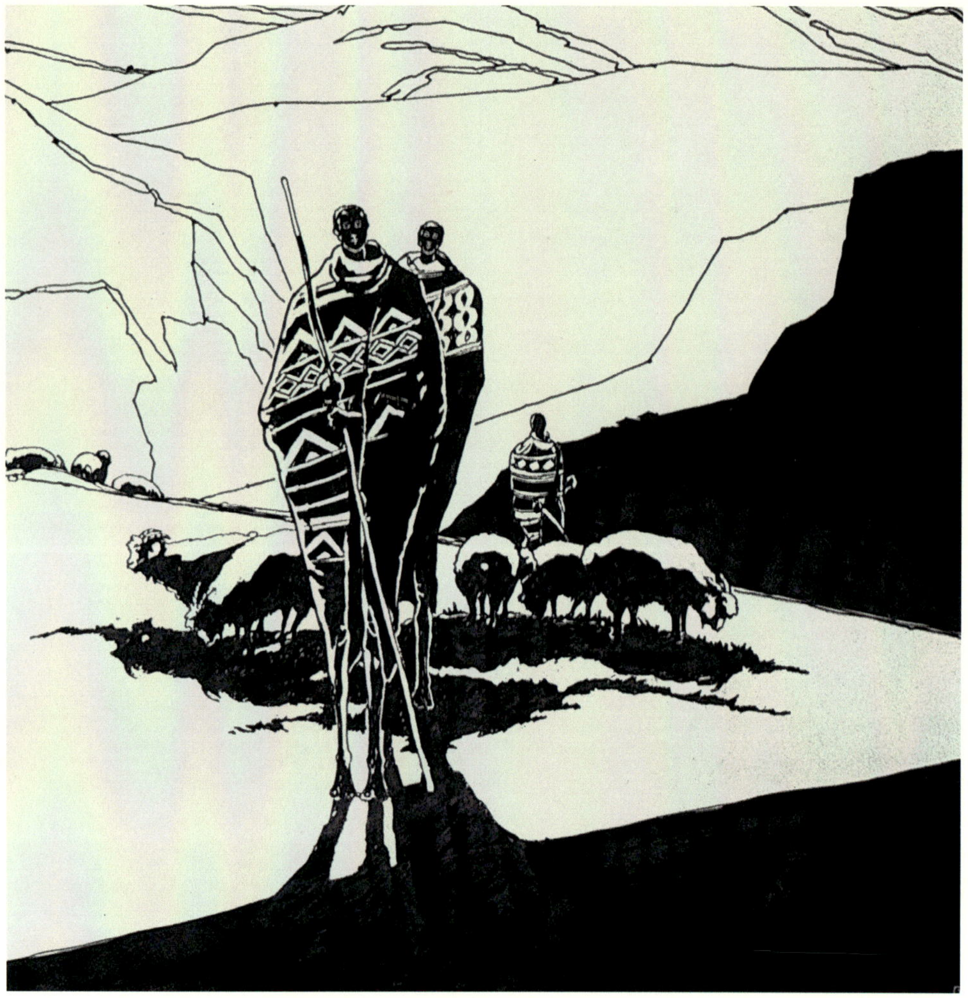

An extract from Tony's Diary

In January of 1980 I first saw the clear hard edged images and silhouettes that make up the Maluti mountains. Although I spent a year travelling and working in Lesotho, one single journey. At the start of the African winter, more than any other, stays in my mind. I saw in a short space of time, many of the colours and changes of Lesotho's landscape.

The weather was unreliable when we left Maseru with its noisy traffic and city life. Maseru contrasts sharply with the rest of Lesotho which is predominantly a land of mountains and silence. It takes a day and a half to drive from Maseru to Qacha's Nek on the Transkei border. I made the trip with John Hurst, a friend who worked in Rural Development. The storm clouds sent shafts of light beaming down on the distant mountains, colouring them in streaks and patches. Later that day the weather changed into the perfect blue skies so common in Southern Africa, bringing a different set of colours and texture to the landscape. We past through (the end of the tarmac roads) and continued on dirt roads down to Mohales Hoek and Moyeni, then up again to Quthing and on to Qach's Nek.

The trip had been full of visual memories, from the herdboys silhouetted on a ridge against the sun, to the mountain villages with smoke from the sweet smelling cow dung fires drifting and falling into valleys joining the clouds. The mountains with their towering peaks, crags, ridges, waterfalls, streams and bridal paths; the Basotho horseman with their blankets and woven grass 'Basotho' hats; the browns and ochres of winter which contrasted with the earlier colours of my visit; the sudden greens after summer storms; the mountain flowers; the silence and the space.

Qacha's Nek is a small remote town, but it has a large Catholic church, a hotel and an old District Commissioners Office and lies on semi-flat land, situated in a pass through the Maluti. After a good meal at the hotel we retired to bed, the weather was turning very cold. When we got up the next morning to make the journey to Sehlabathebe National Park, it was snowing. We decided to forget the planned trip and return to Maseru. The snow brought out many new and different colours I had not seen before.

After two hours of driving we were stuck firmly in the snow and it was only my companion's resourcefulness that got us going again. Two hours later we were out of the snow and back in sunshine - the snow had gone, the weather was sunny. It often changes between one range of mountains and the next. I remember looking down on a village, the fields were ploughed in a spiral and the snow lay between furrows of red earth throwing them into startling contrast. We pressed on to Mount Moososi to camp by a small waterfall and continued the next day to Maseru.

Visits to Marakabei 'The Blue Mountain Pass', Thaba Basiu the 'Mountain of Night', Bushman's Pass, Morija and many other places brought me more visual ideas - my mind was becoming full of images.

I made a decision to keep working at the studio in Maseru that I shared with my old friend Peter Hayes. After seven months work I had an exhibition of over fifty paintings and drawings at The Hilton Hotel in Maseru. It was a great success.

Further travels took me to Zululand, Swaziland and several other parts of Southern Africa, then on to Zimbabwe and Kenya.

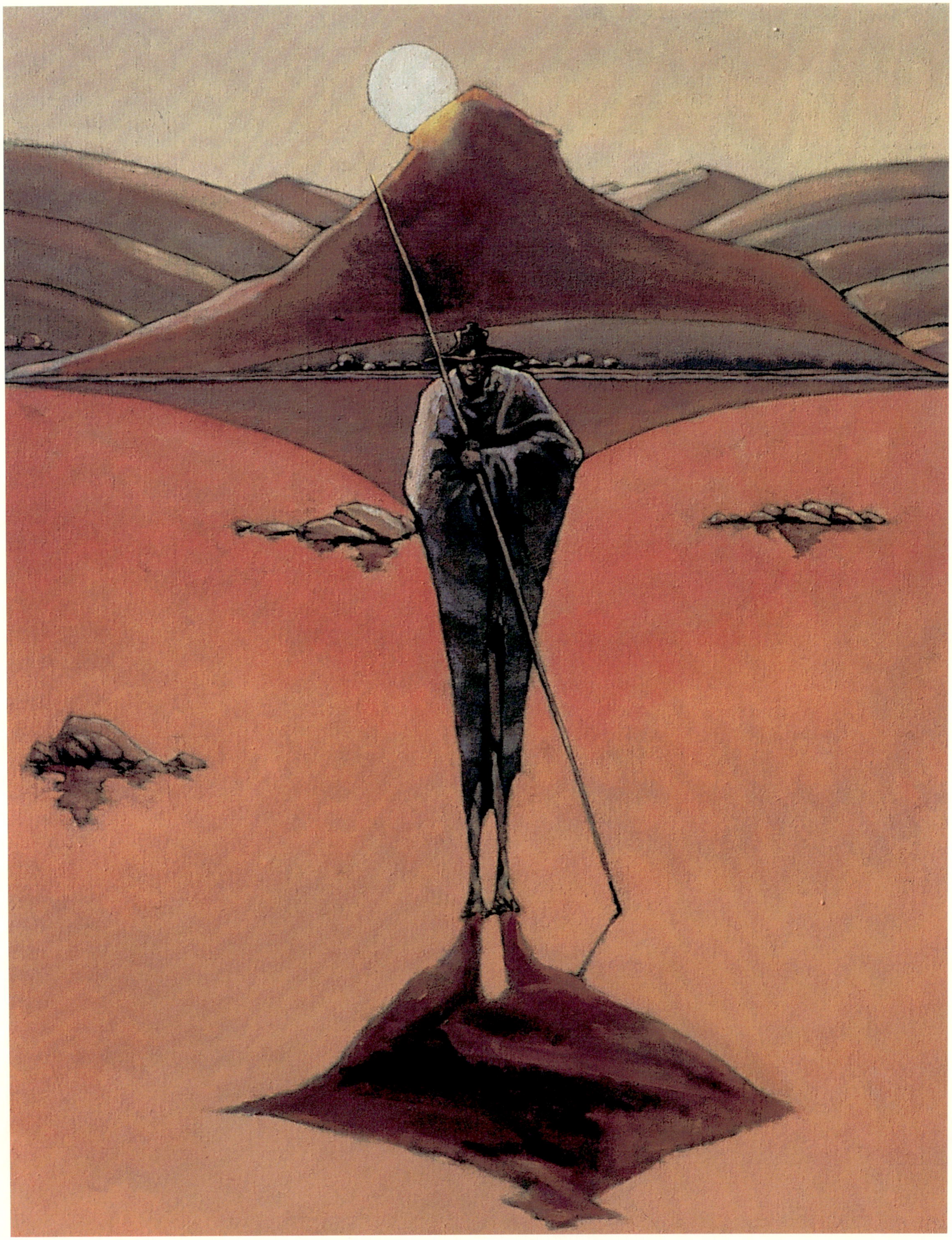

Opposite page: ***Protecting the Flocks -*** *Protected by the mountains behind and the herdboys in front, the sheep and goats graze safely in the deepening shadows of early evening.(Ink)*
Left: ***At One -*** *The unity between man and his mountains is a constant theme explored by Tony in his work. To an outsider the rugged mountains seem unforgiving and inhospitable, but to the Basotho they are a symbol of life and eternity. (Acrylic)*

People of Africa

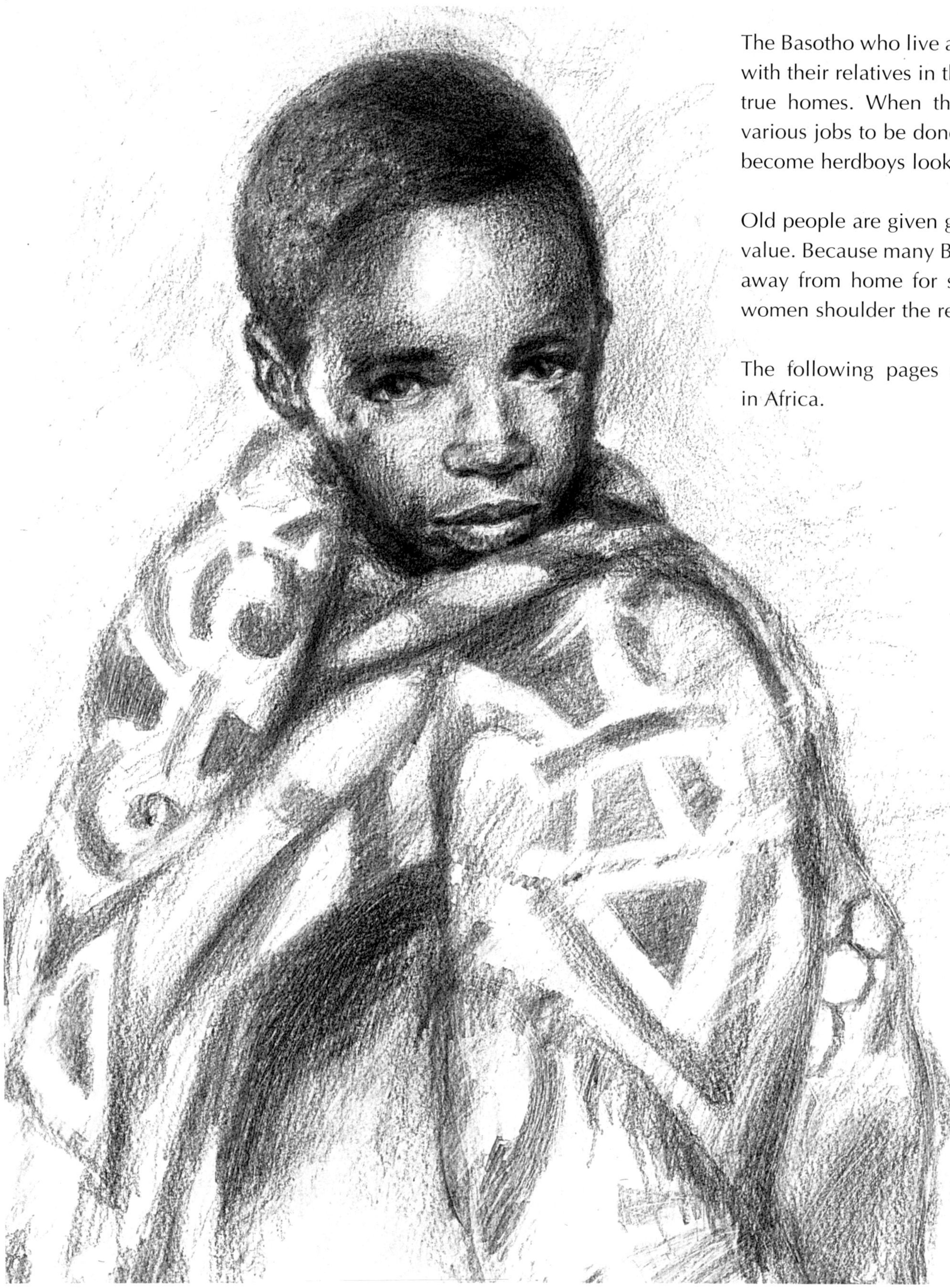

The Basotho who live and work in the towns of Lesotho retain very strong ties with their relatives in the rural villages, often regarding these villages as their true homes. When the children become of age, they help out with the various jobs to be done in the village. Starting from the age of five, the boys become herdboys looking after the cattle, sheep and goats.

Old people are given great respect by the village and their advice is of great value. Because many Basotho men work in the mines of South Africa they are away from home for several months at a time. Left at home, the Basotho women shoulder the responsibility of the children's upbringing.

The following pages show Tony's colourful interpretation of the people in Africa.

Innocence - *Boys leave home at an early age to watch over the family herds of sheep and goats as they graze on chilly mountain slopes. It's an often cold and lonely life. (Pencil)*

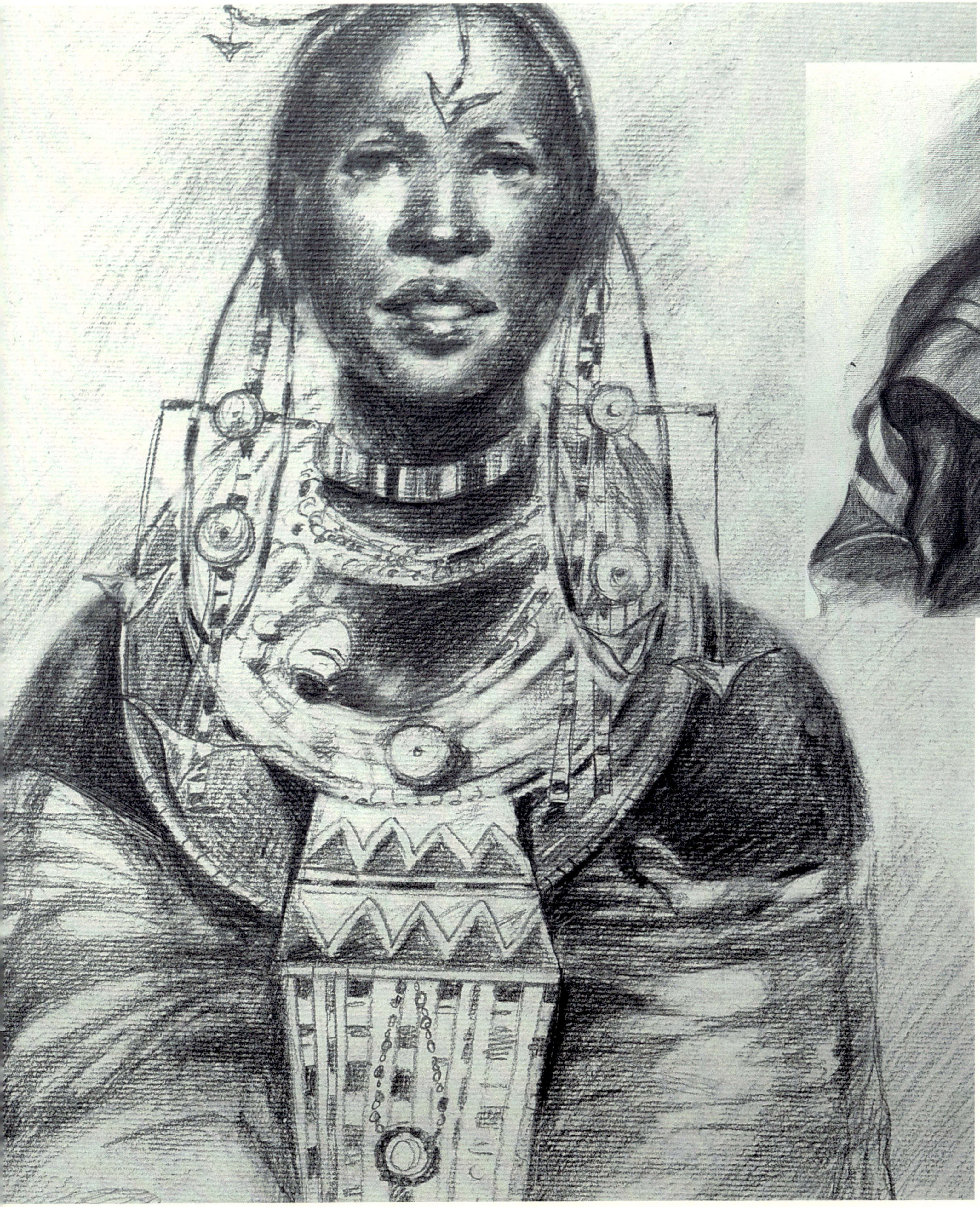

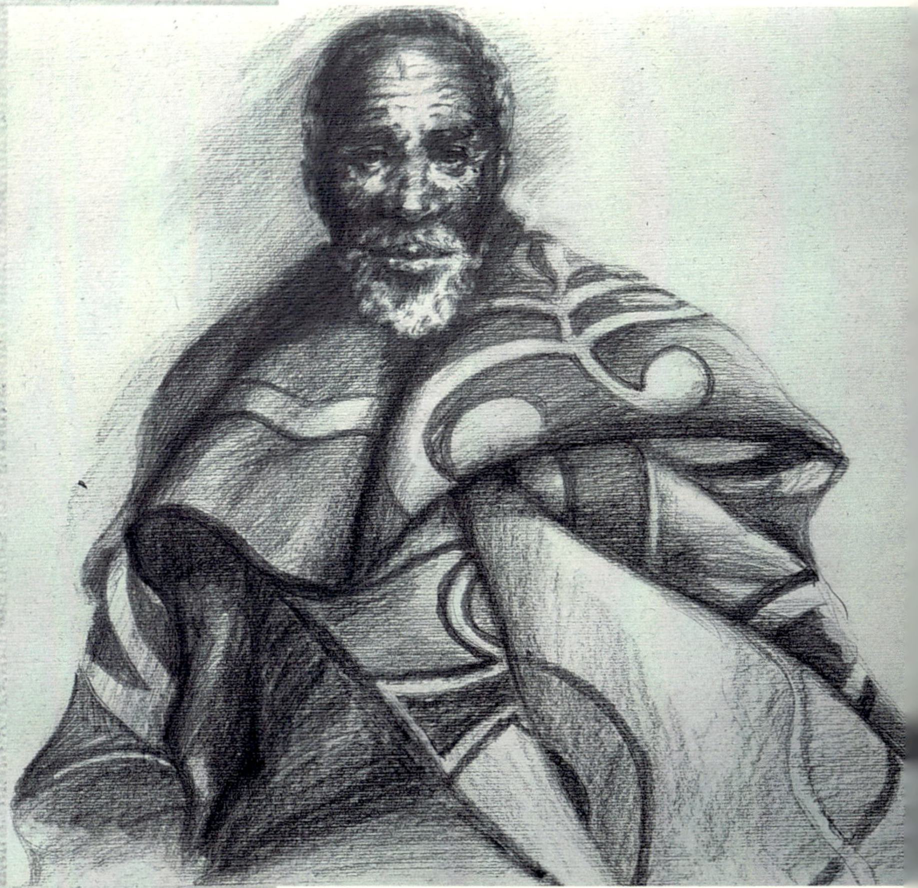

Portrait of an Old Man **-** *This richly decorated blanket gives strength and dignity to an old man in his declining years as he contemplates his past.*
(Pencil)

Maasai Bride **-** *Dressed in her finest jewellery on her wedding day, this Maasai girl looks bravely ahead as she walks towards her new home. To look back at her old home would bring bad luck in her new life.*
(Pencil)

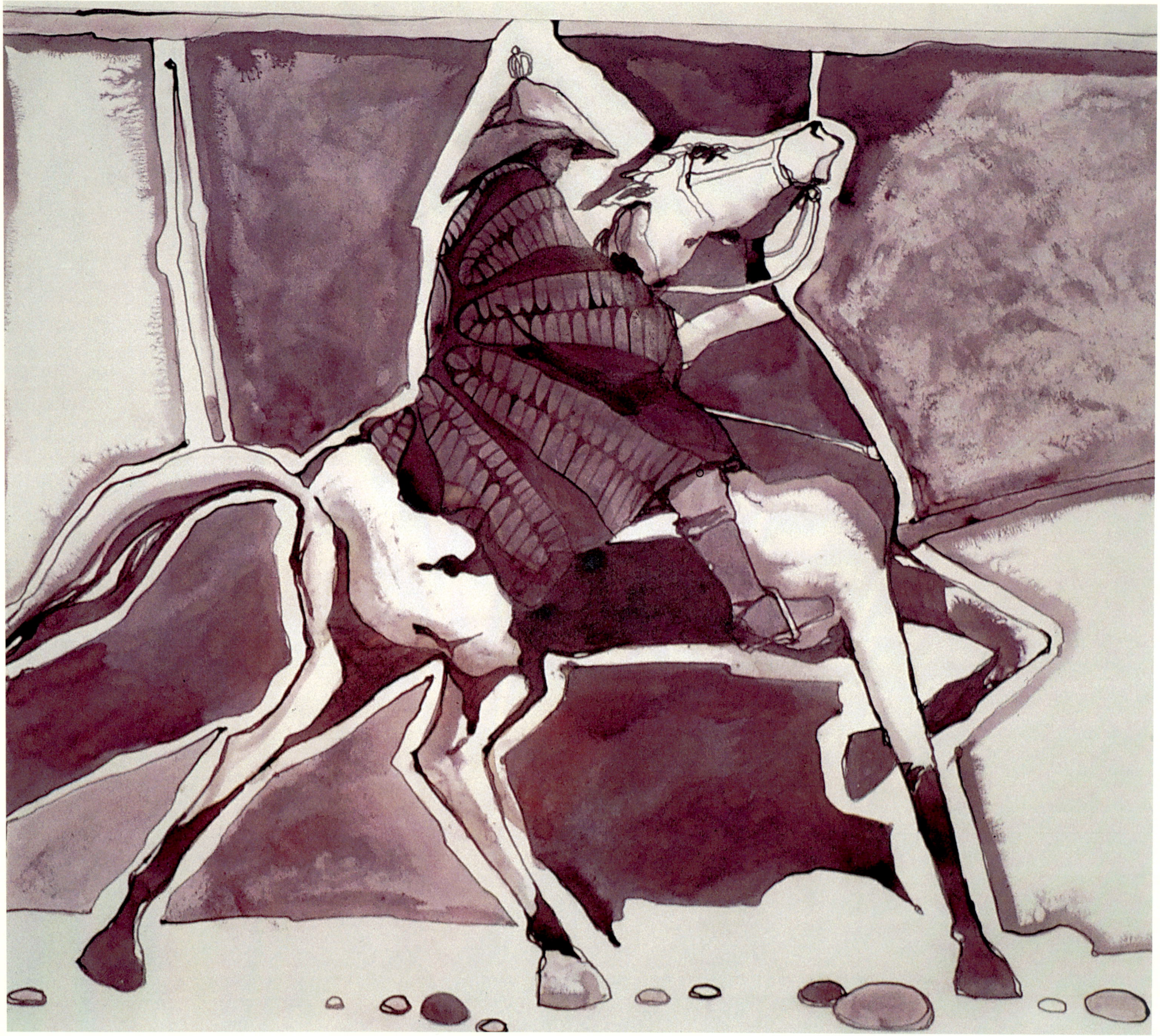

Riding Right - *Bonded, strong and fearless, the Mosotho rider and his horse face constant hazards with courage and pride.*
(Ink wash)

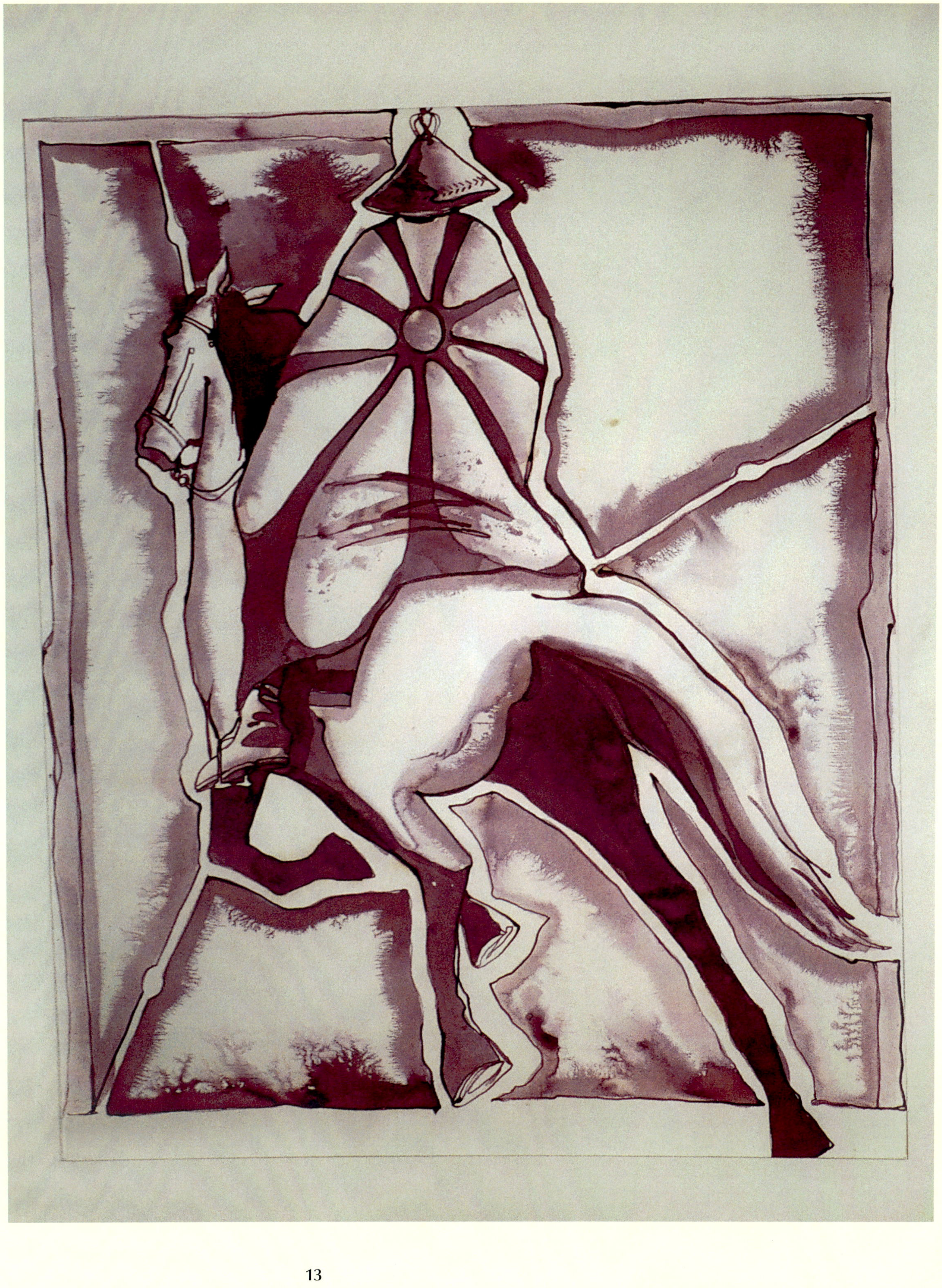

Riding Left - *With the bold design of a rising sun on his back, the rider and his sturdy mount ride off to face unknown dangers.*
(Ink wash)

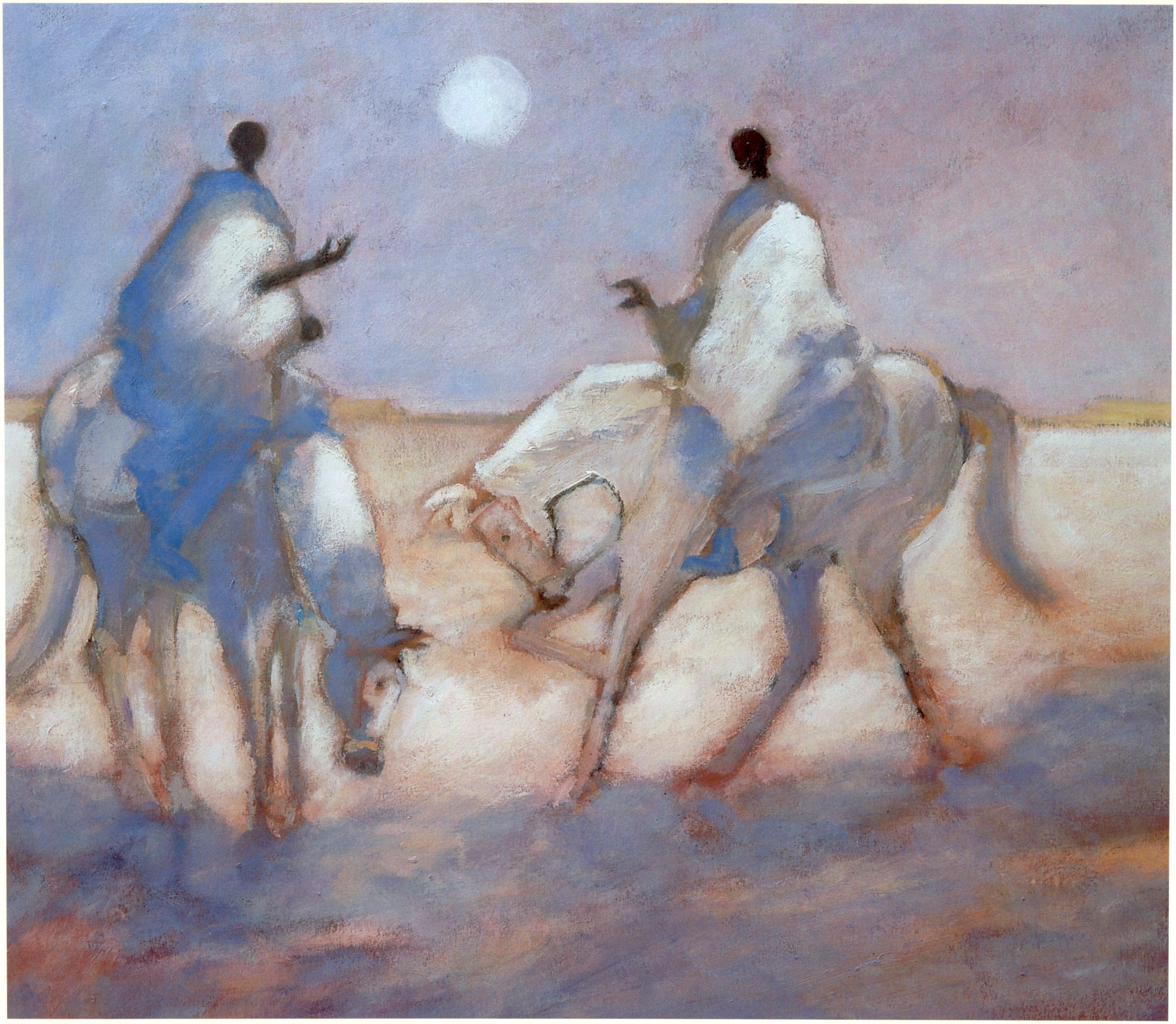

Dawn Greeting - *Two horsemen exchange traditional greetings and news in the cold, blue light of early dawn. While travelling on long and lonely journeys, a little companionship along the way is most welcome.*
(Pastel)

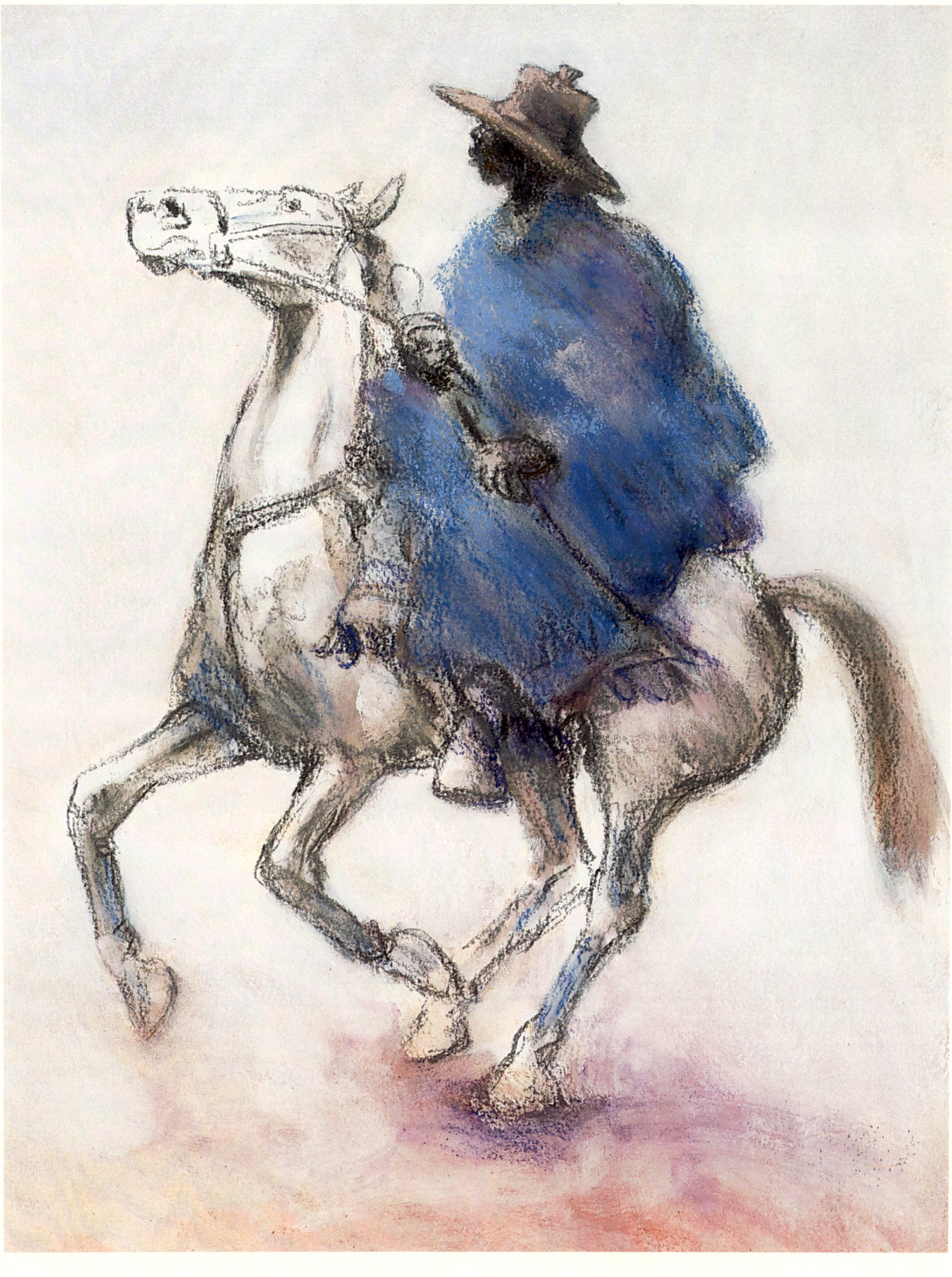

Companions - *The Mosotho horseman builds a special bond with his travelling companion. Together they will cross many mountain ranges, each dependent on the other for a safe arrival.*
(Pastel)

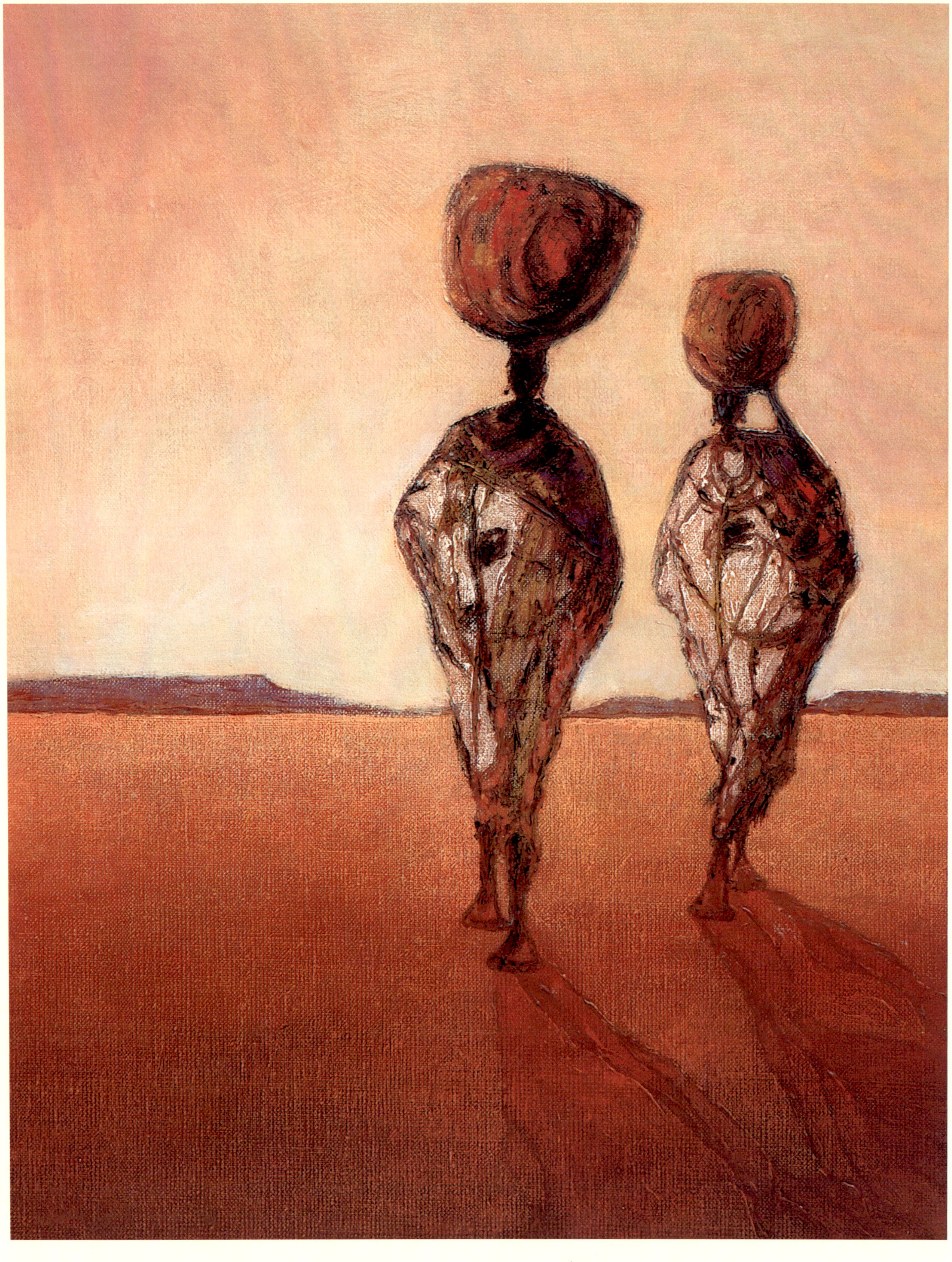

Going Home - *Carrying new life on their backs and water, the continuation of life on their heads, the women walk home in the knowledge that their work is done for the day.*
(Acrylic)

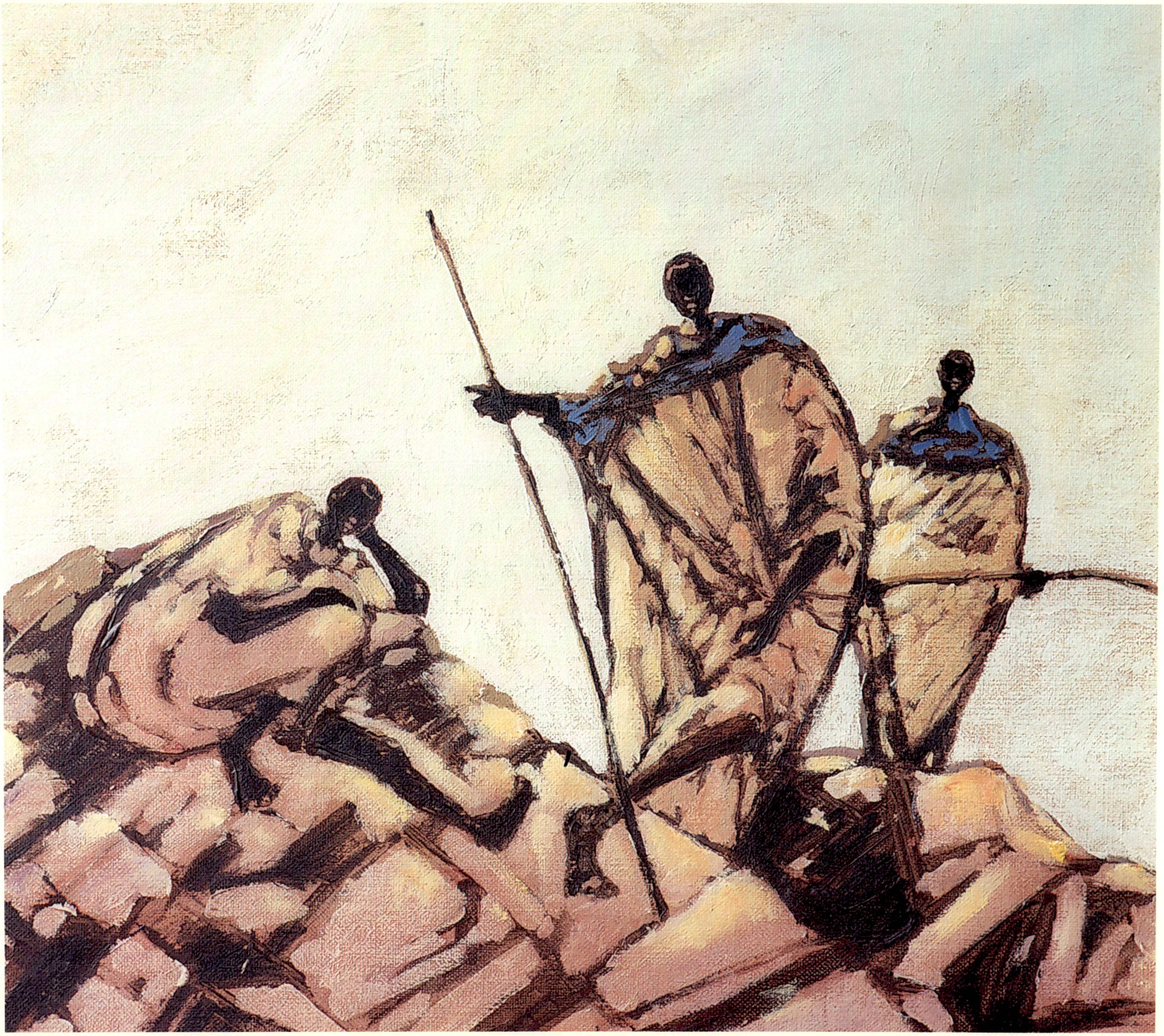

At the Summit - *While two figures stand silhouetted against the clear mountain skies, another is so much a part of his surroundings that he is camouflaged against the rocks. (Acrylic)*

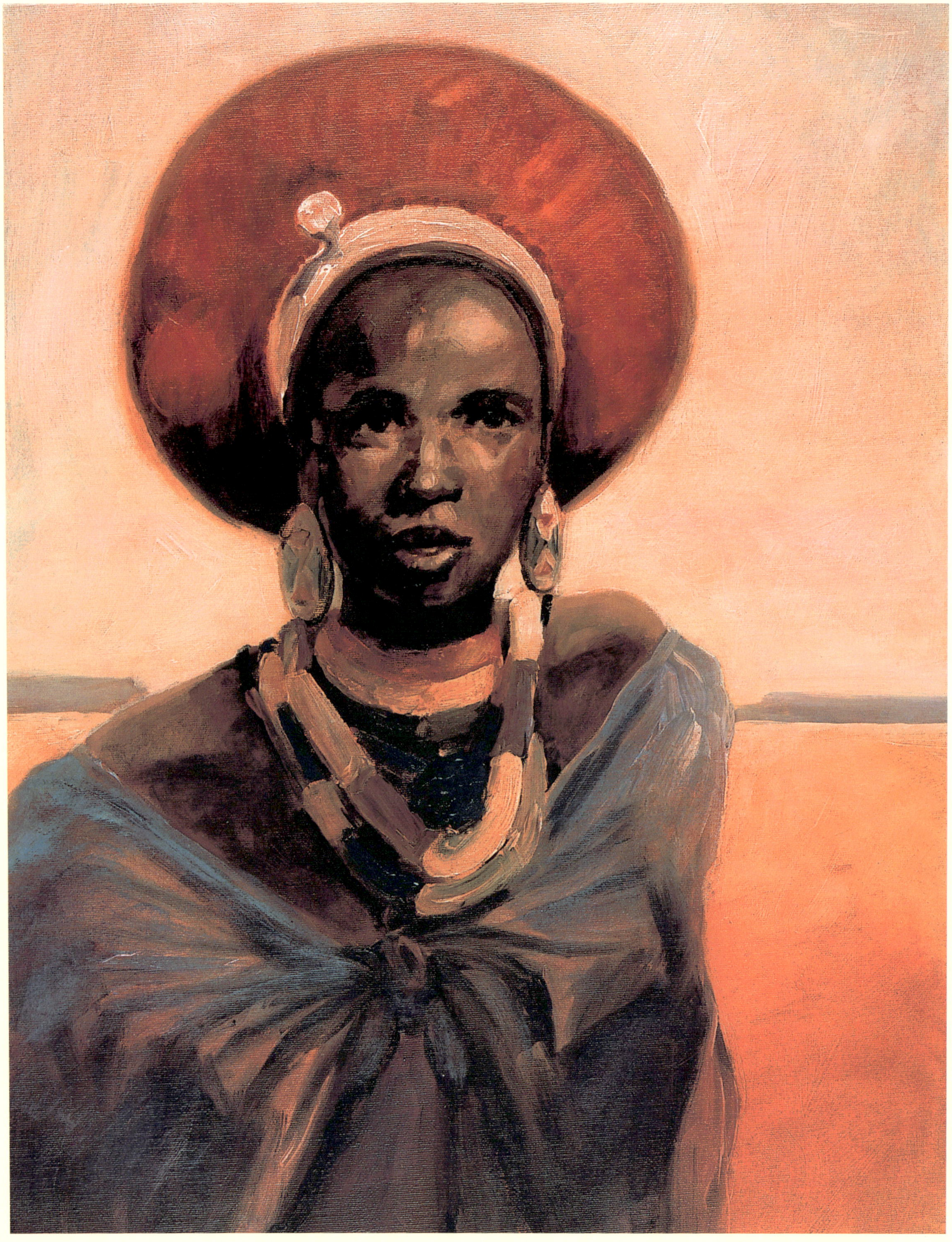

Zulu Girl - *The traditional Zulu woman epitomises the elegance and grace of African women everywhere. Adorned with vibrant beaded jewellery, she shines against the landscape of her homeland. (Acrylic)*

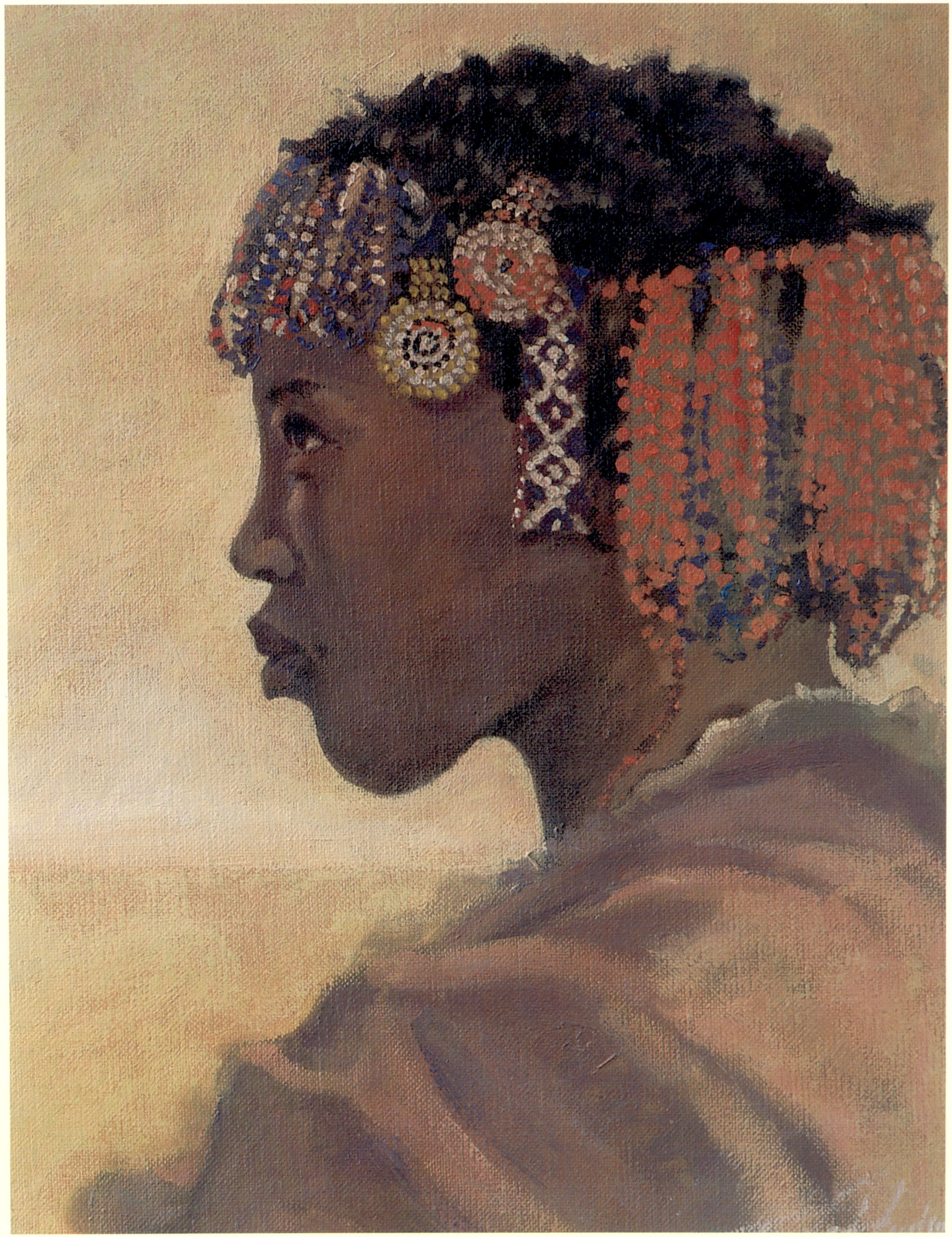

Sunni - *Clothing is often cool and simple in Africa, but women across the continent find alluring ways to make themselves attractive with fascinating hair plating and jewellery.*
(Acrylic)

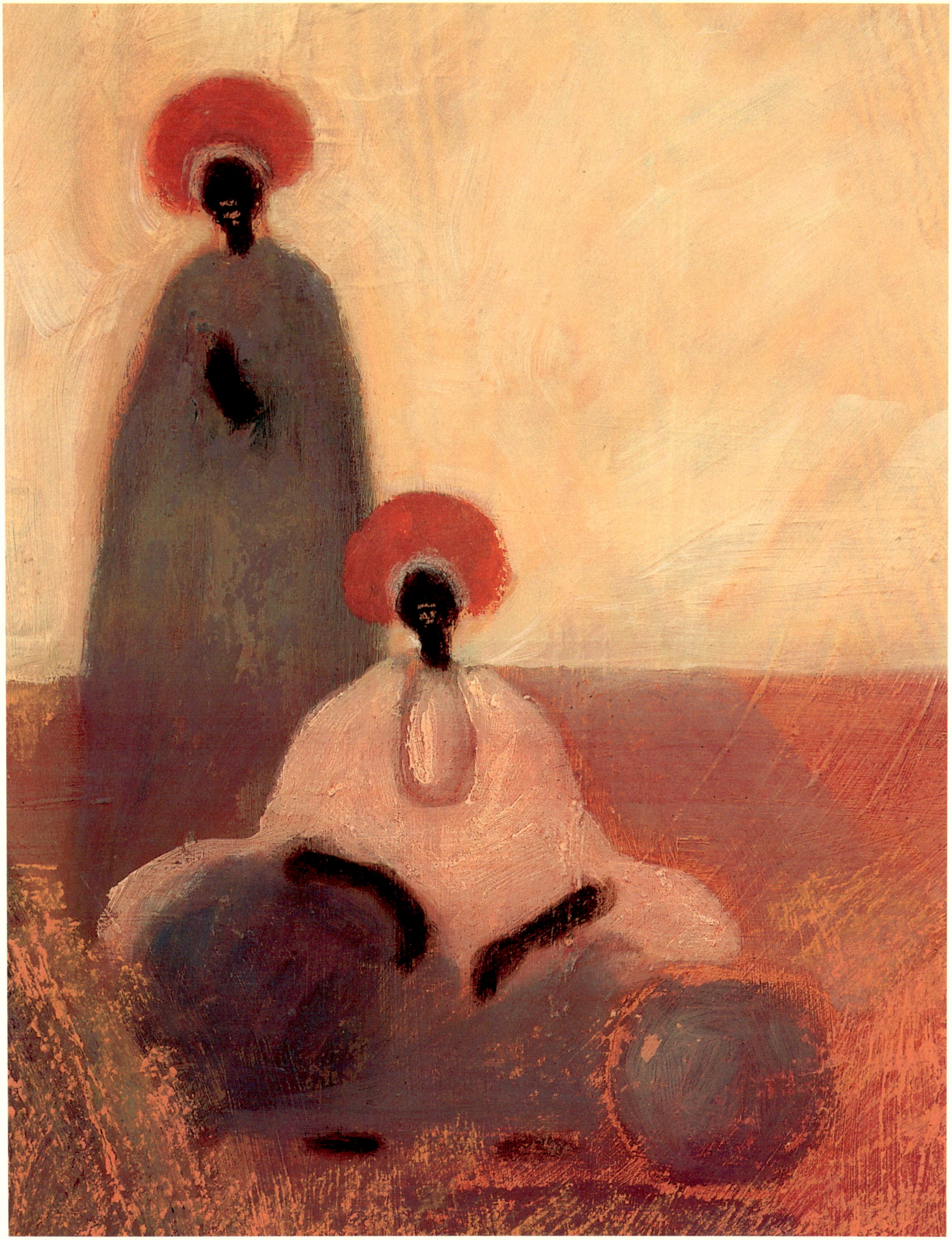

Tembu Potters **-** *Women guard the cycle of life. Through childbirth and the creation of symmetrical pots in which to store life-giving water, the women of Africa ensure that life continues.*
(Acrylic)

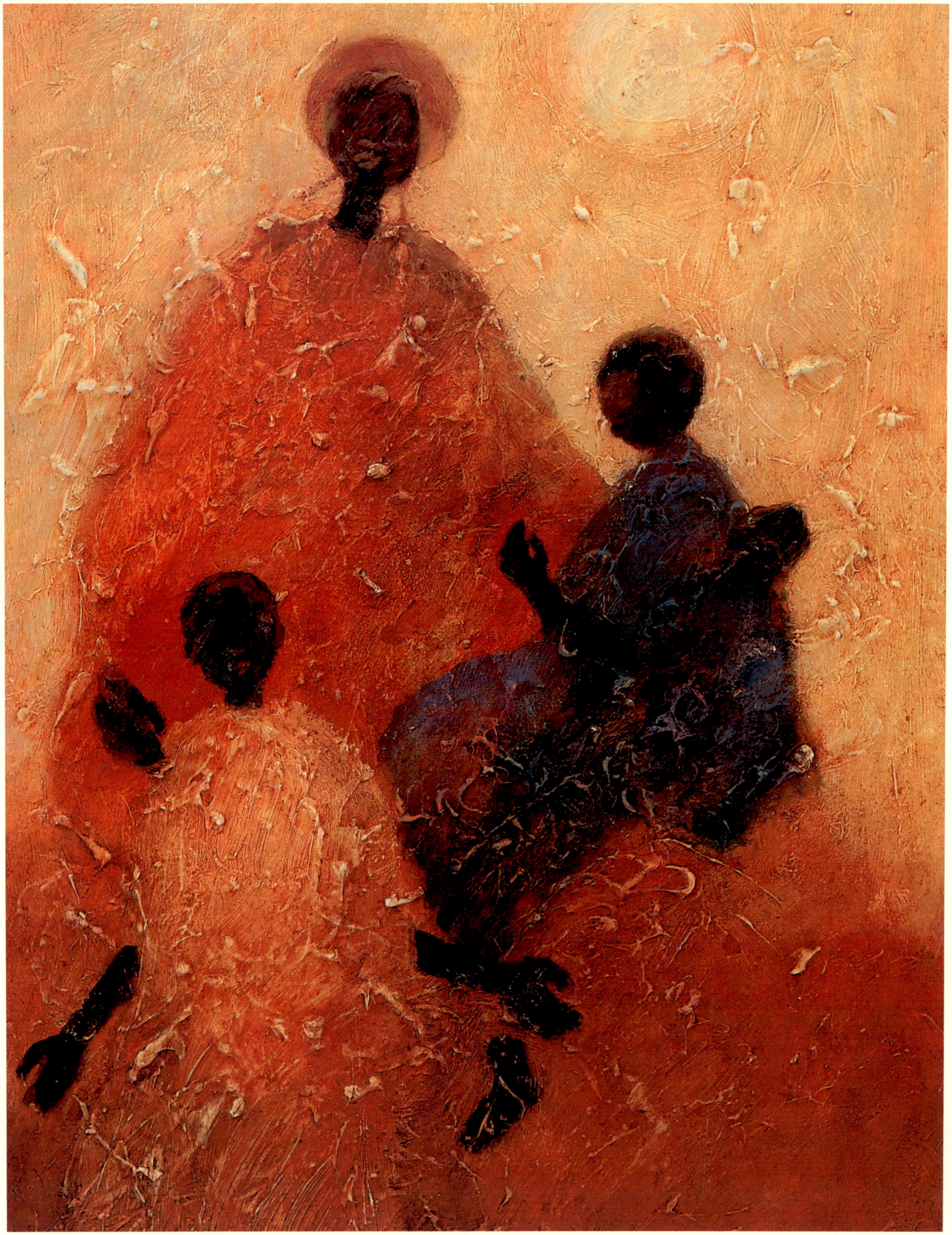

Motherhood - *Enveloped by the protective frame of their mother, two children shelter from the harshness of reality as they grow in the warmth of her love and the heat of the African sun. (Acrylic)*

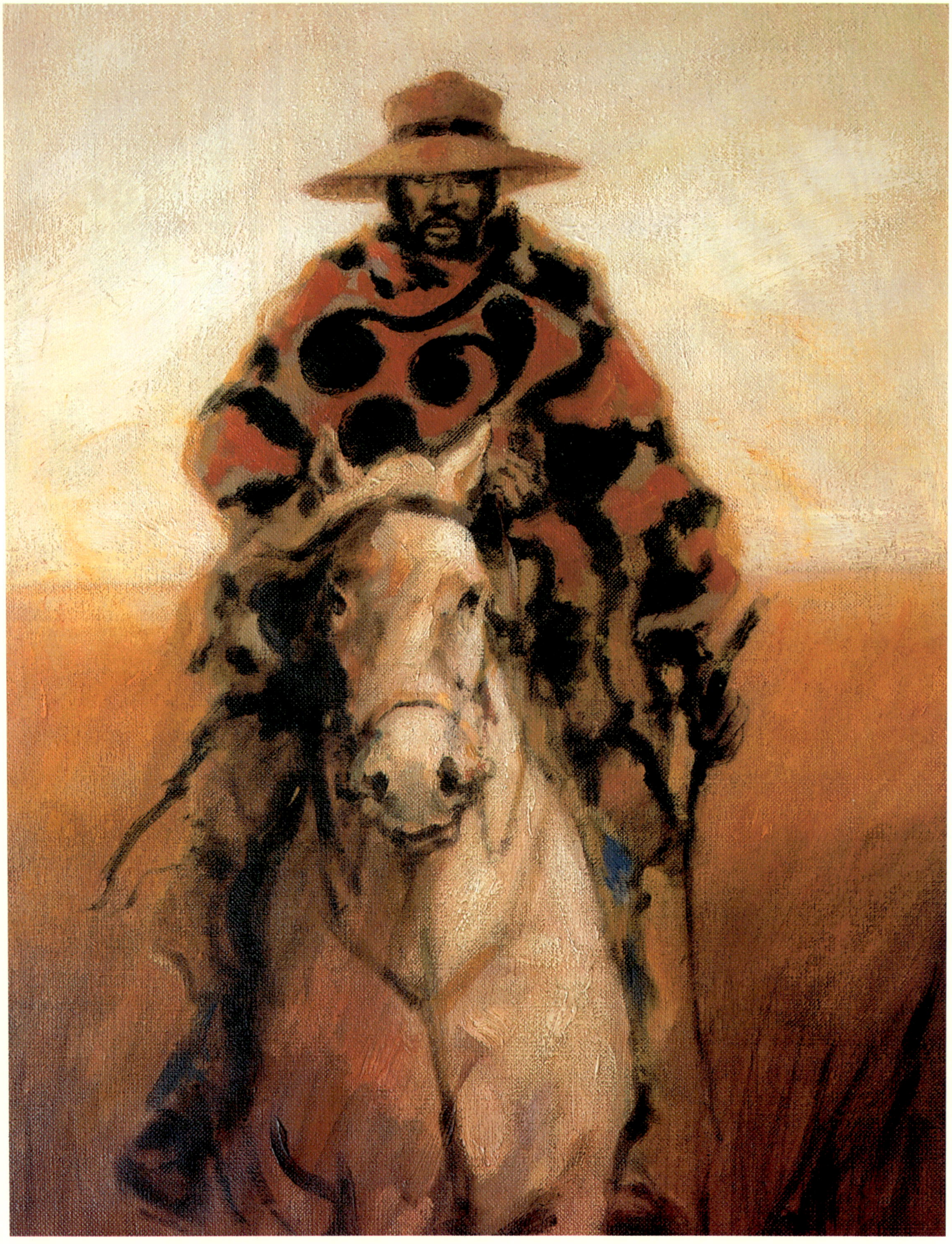

A Sotho Horseman - *The high mountains of Lesotho are cold and remote with few roads and many flowing streams of clear water. Riding their hardy Basotho ponies, the men will travel far afield in search of food and work. They keep out the cold by wearing thick blankets and distinctive straw hats.*
(Acrylic)

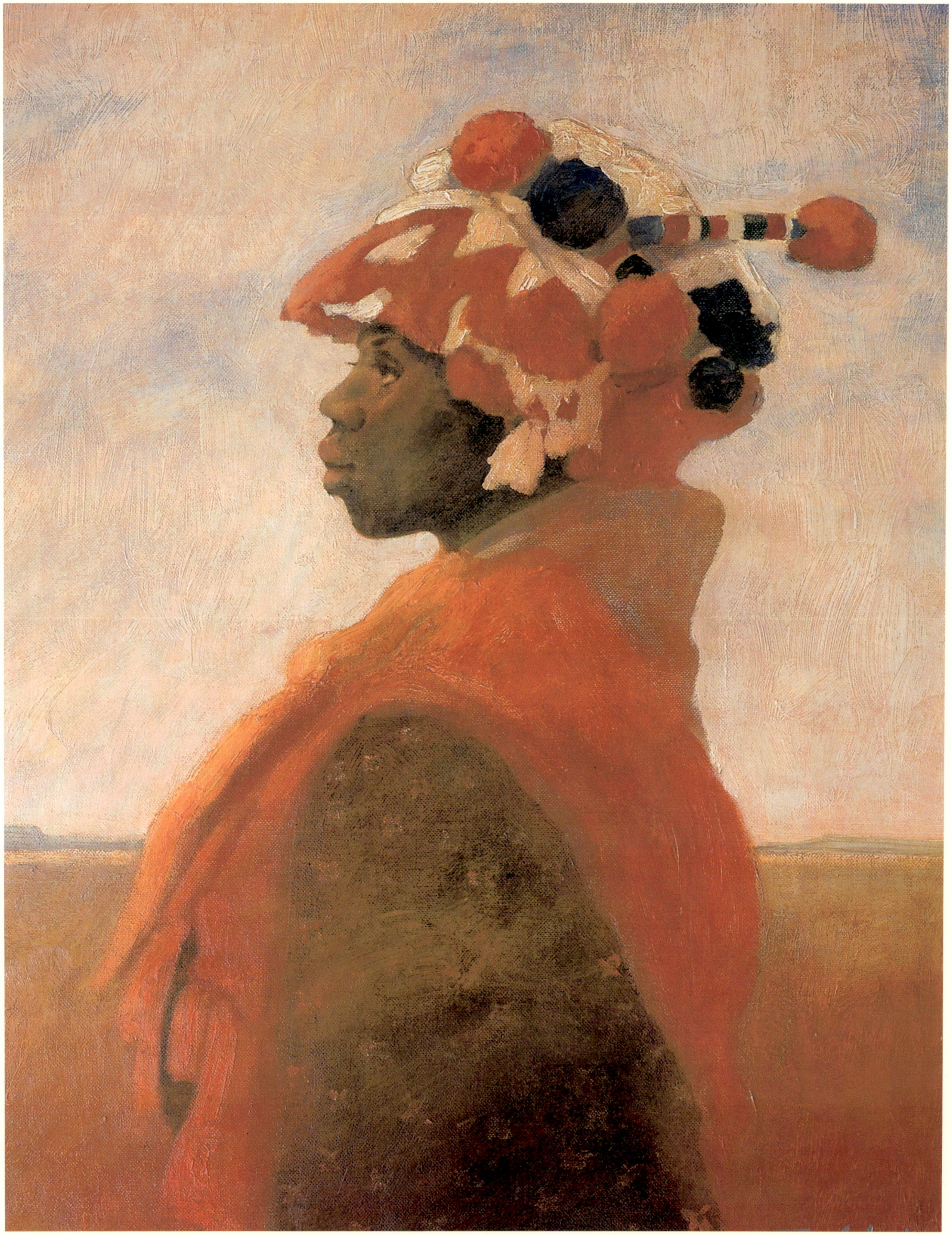

Zulu woman - *Aware of their important role in life, women can be as elegant, proud and haughty as any queen.*
(Acrylic)

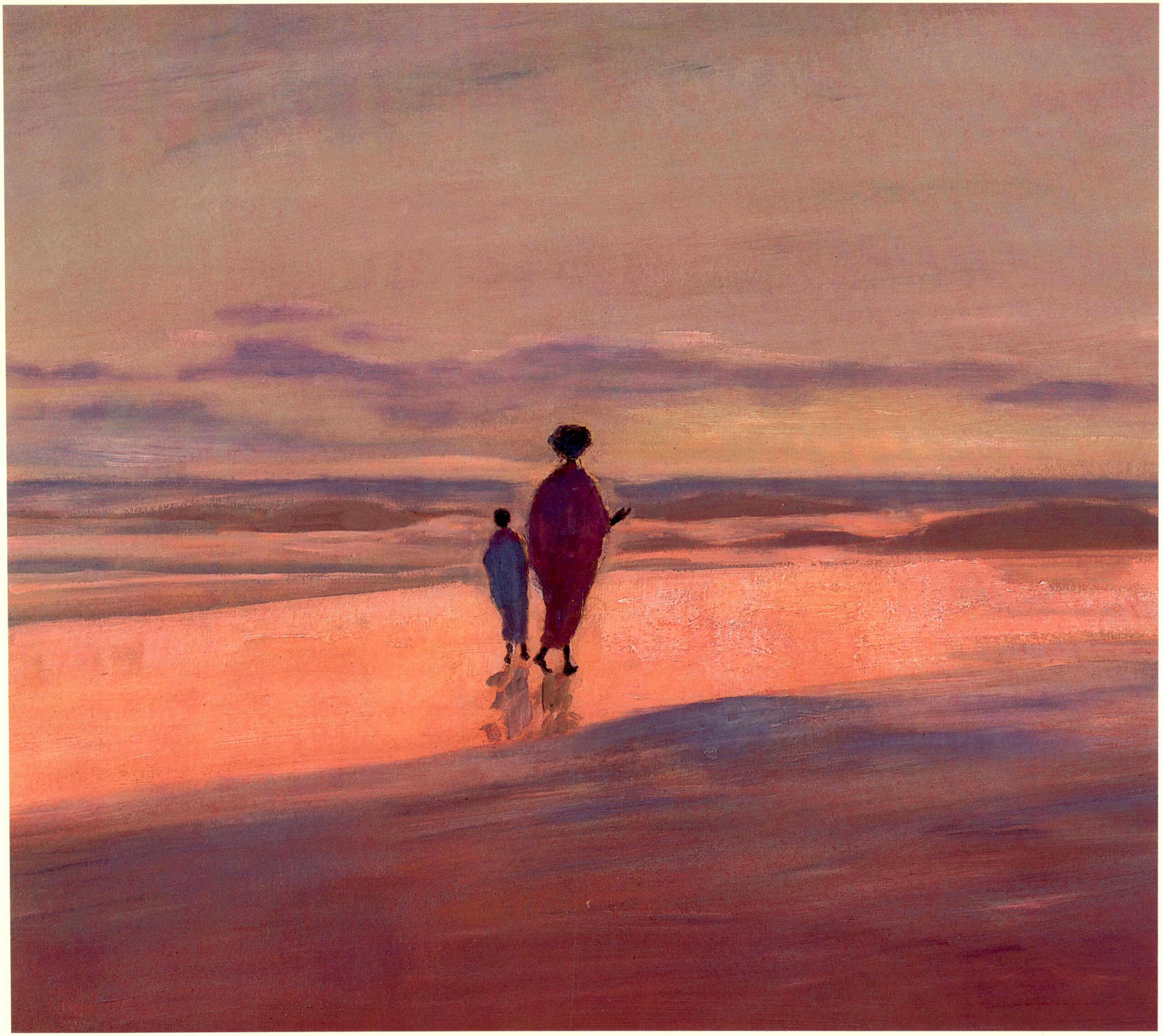

Above: ***In the Distance*** *- The vast skies and natural elements of Africa are a constant reminder of the fragility and insignificance of human life. (Acrylic) Opposite page:* ***The Piper*** *- From the frail reed pipe emerges a song of harmony between man and his world. Music makes the shadows recede and the warmth circulate around the piper as he plays a lament for the passing day. (Acrylic)*

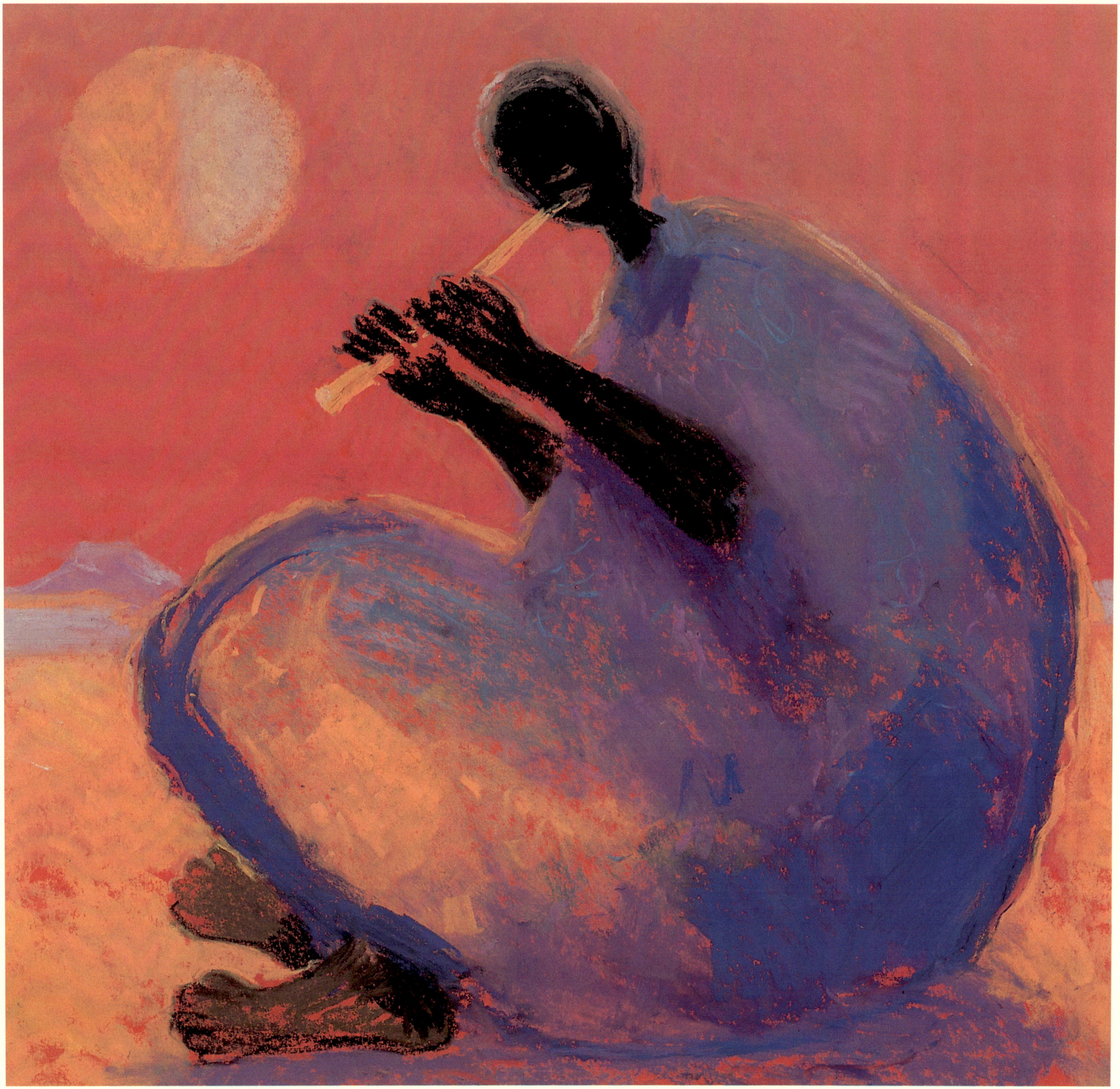

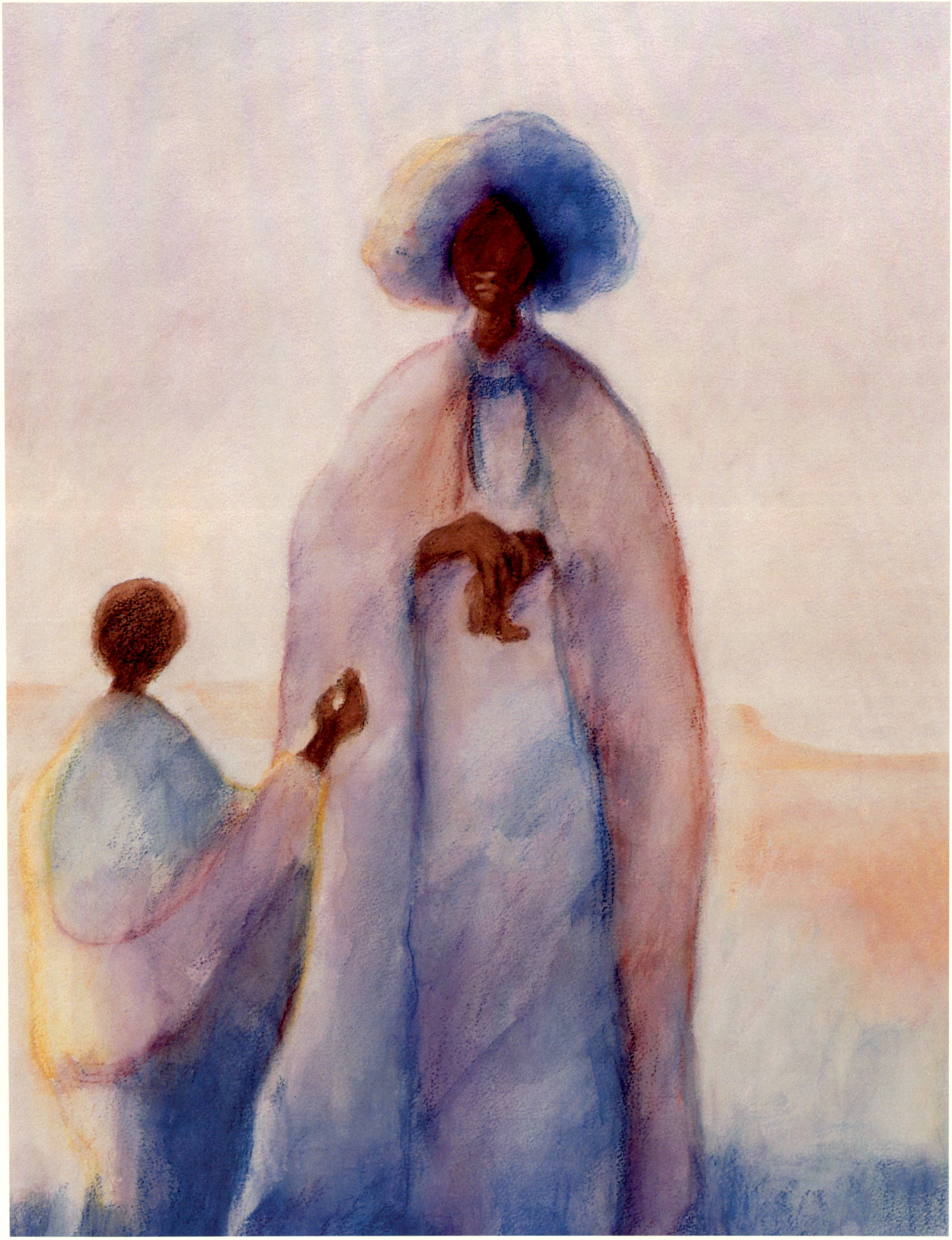

Blue Morning - *The spiritual bonding of a mother and her children is universal. (Pastel & Watercolour)*

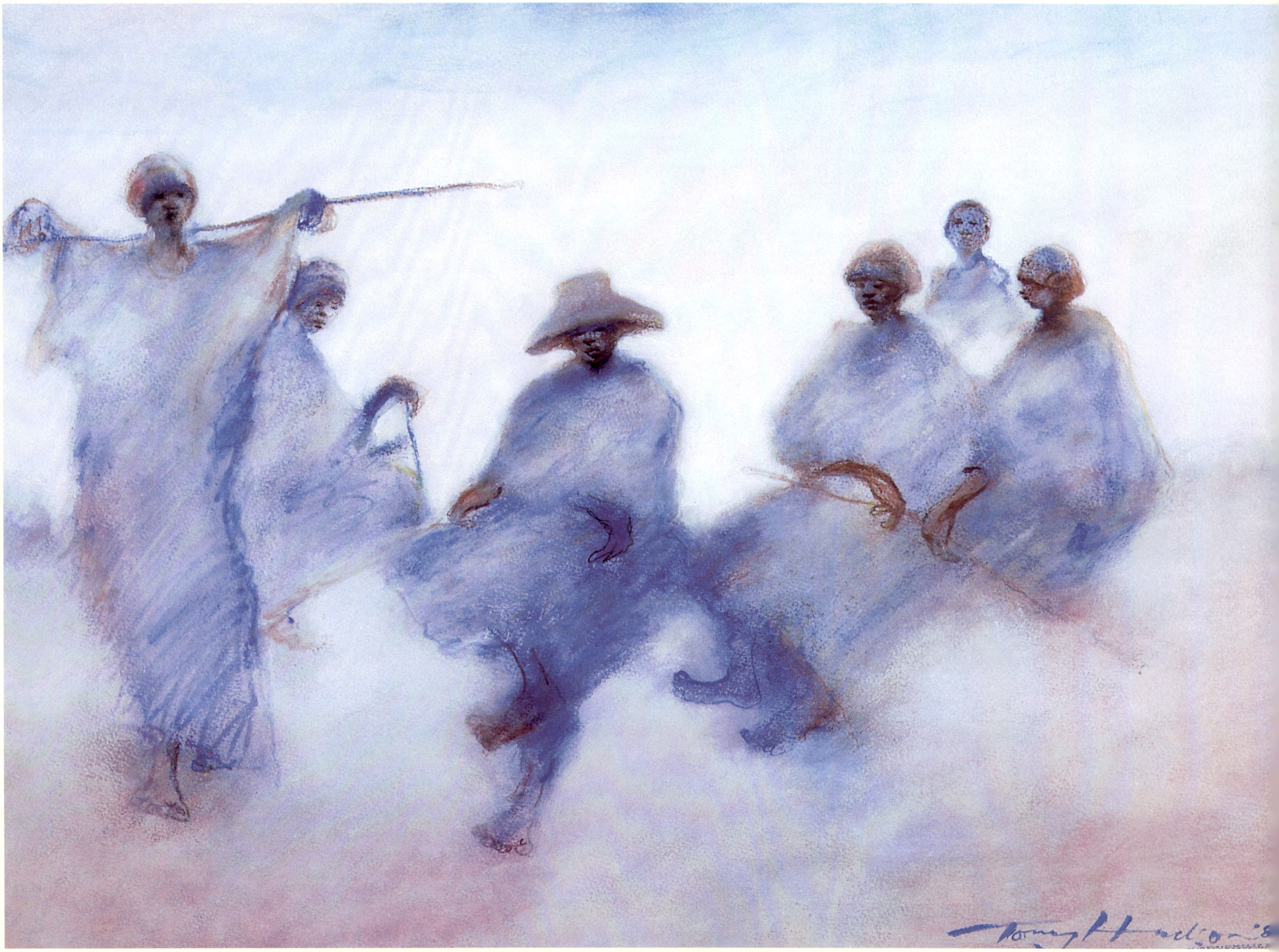

***Herdboys** - High in the mountains of Lesotho, young men learn to care for the flocks of sheep and goats which represent the wealth of their families. Often illiterate, they are nevertheless well versed in the ways of survival and animal husbandry. (Pastel & Watercolour)*

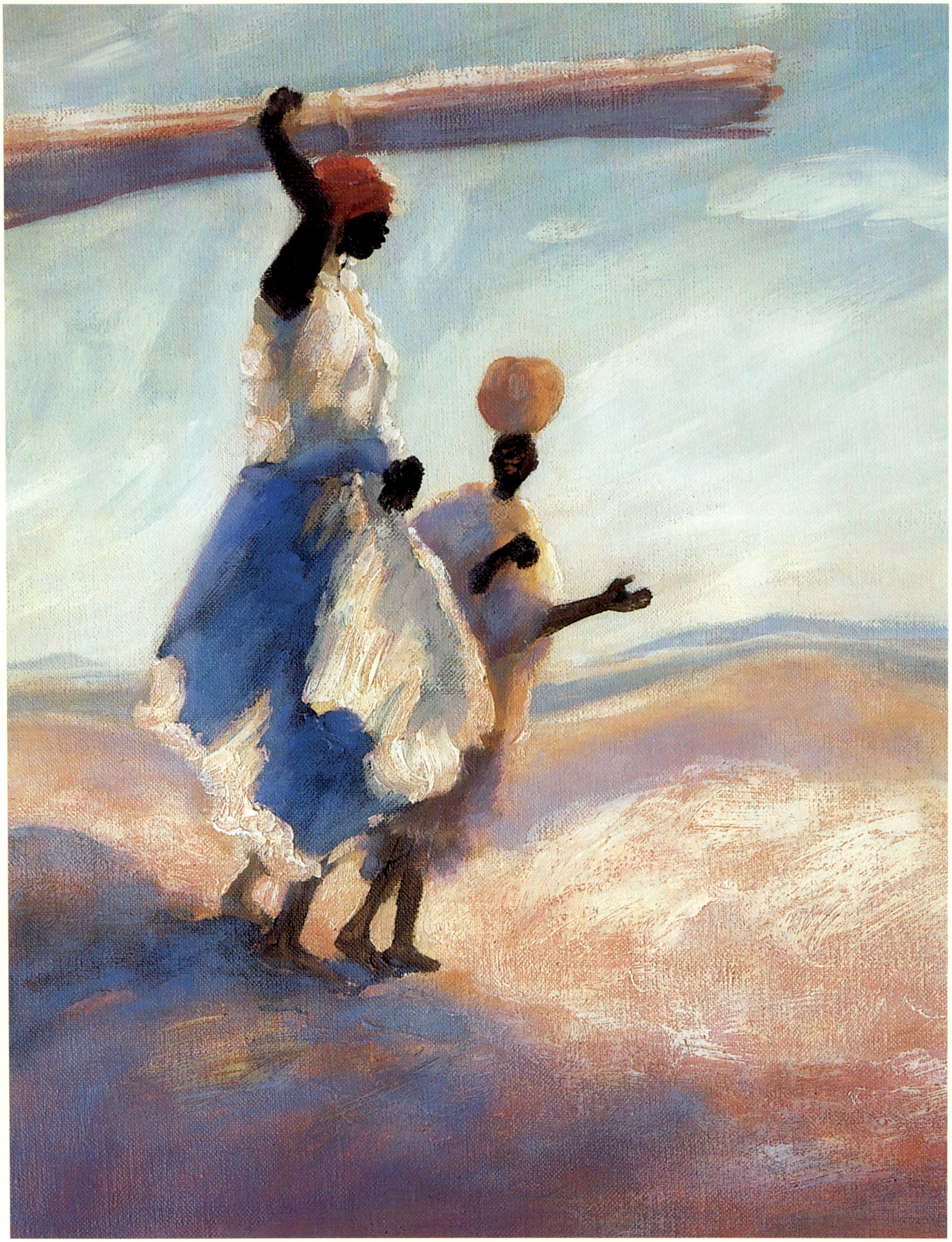

***Wood Carrying -** As the trees around the homestead are cut down, the women must walk further and further to fetch wood, while they may face many dangers on the way. The land too is in danger of degradation.*
(Acrylic)

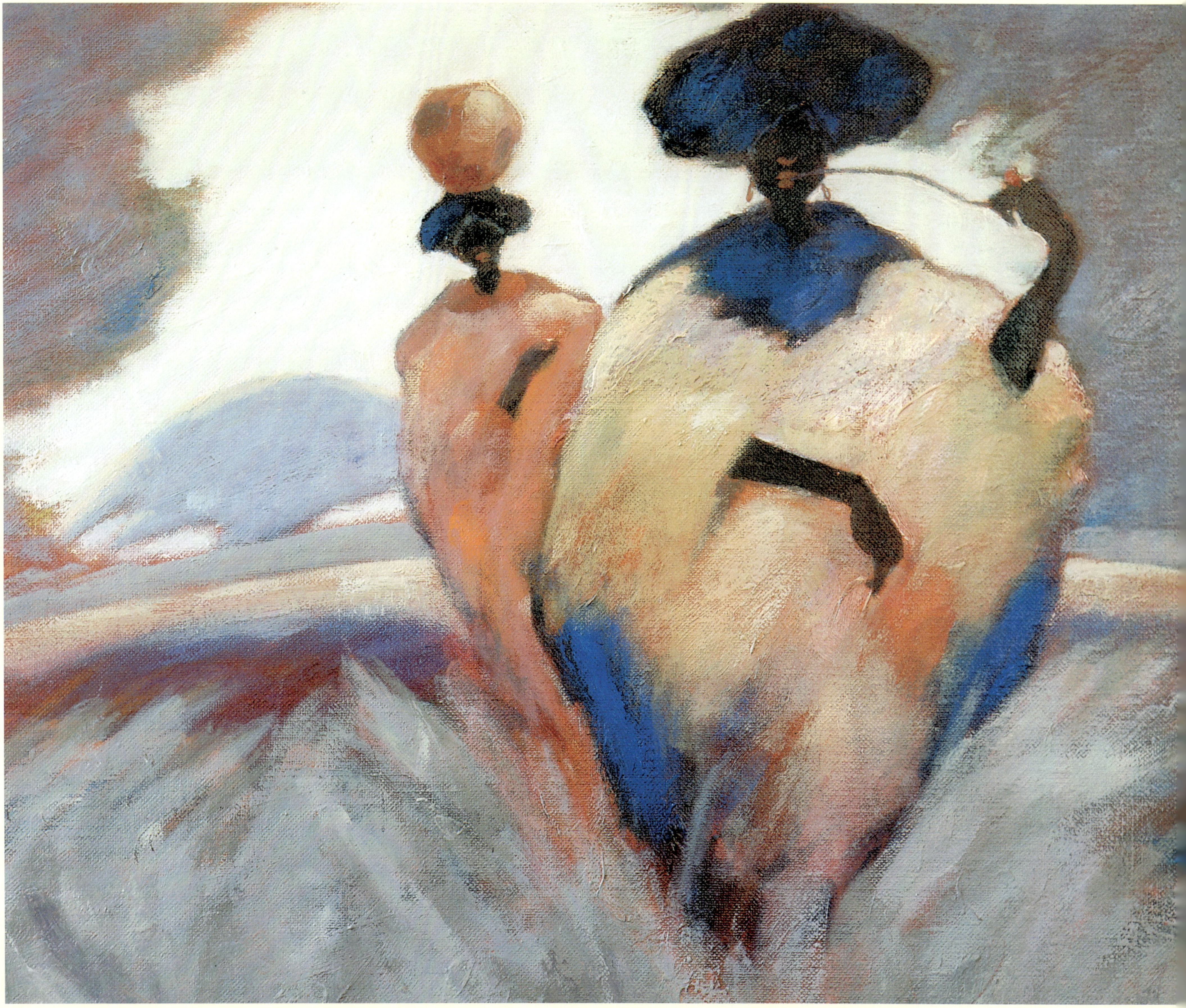

***Misty Morning** - Illuminated by an ethereal light, these ghostly shapes emerge through the mist as they begin the day's chores. (Pastel)*

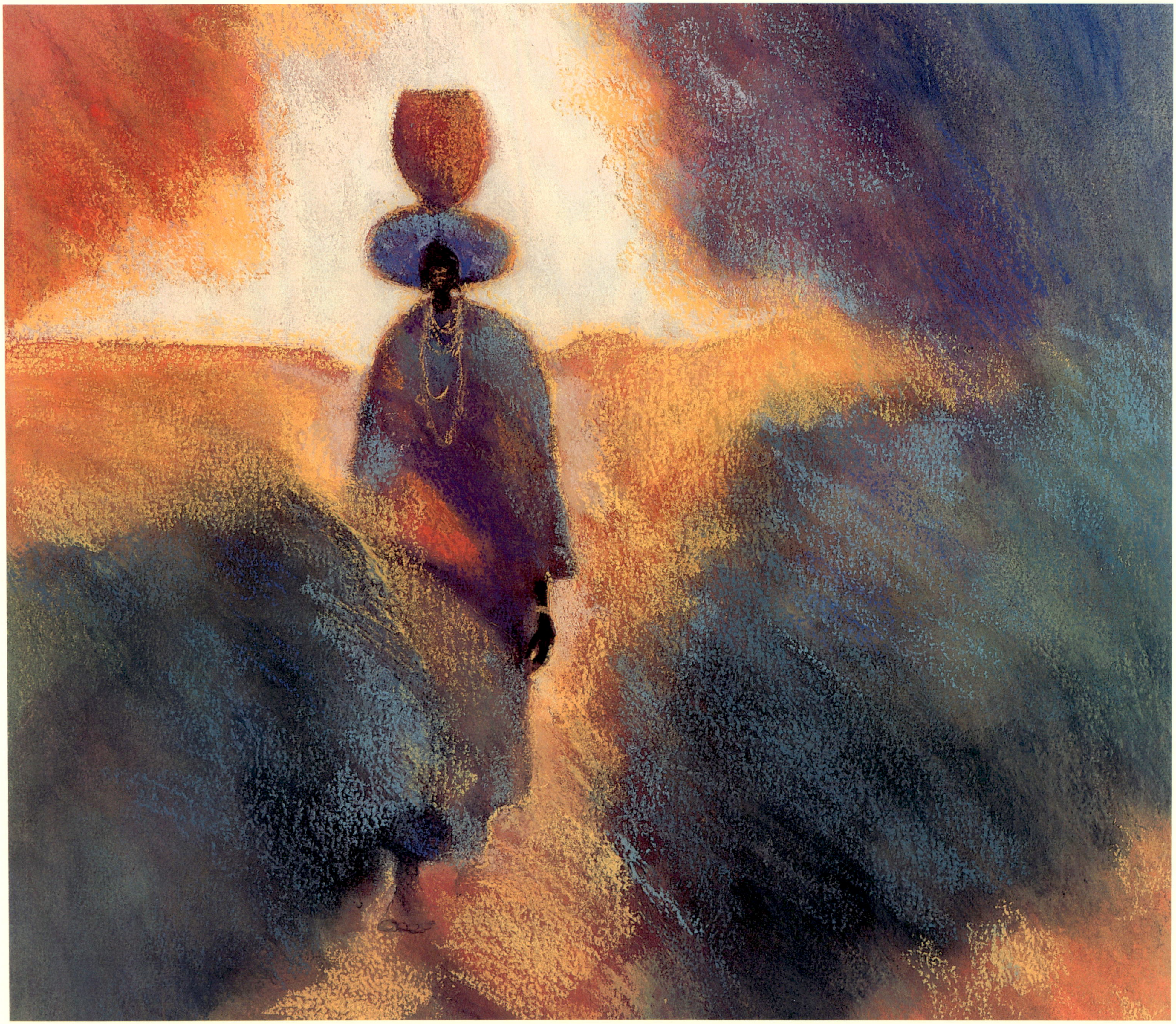

Above: ***Fetching Water*** *- Whatever dark clouds may enter our lives, the simple image of a woman carrying water to her family must represent the epitome of survival. (Pastel) Opposite page:* ***Tembu Tranquillity*** *- The Tembu live on the coastal plains of southern Africa where the climate is temperate and the grass is plentiful after the rains. Living in harmony with each other and their environment, they present a united image of contentment. (Pastel)*

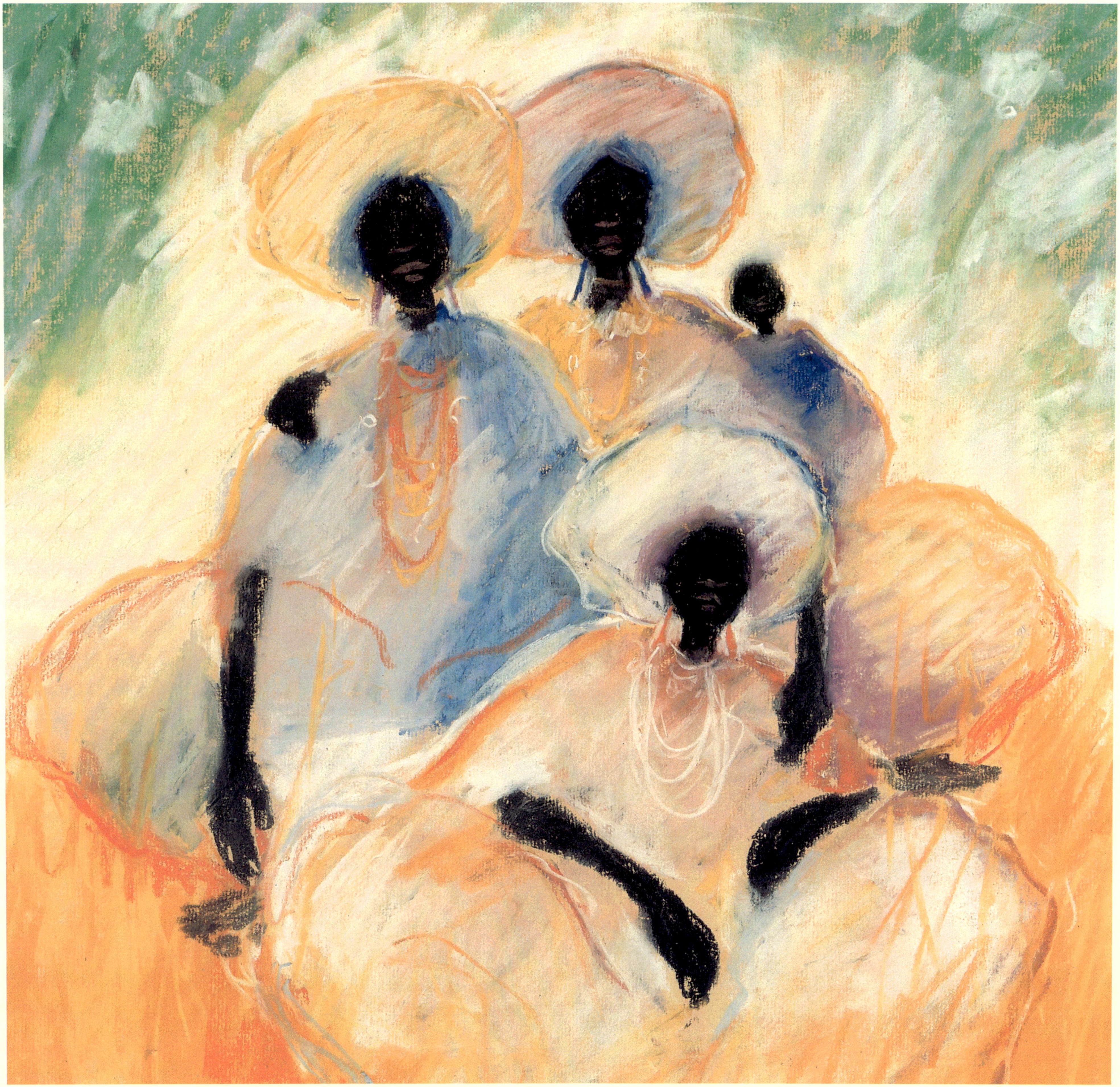

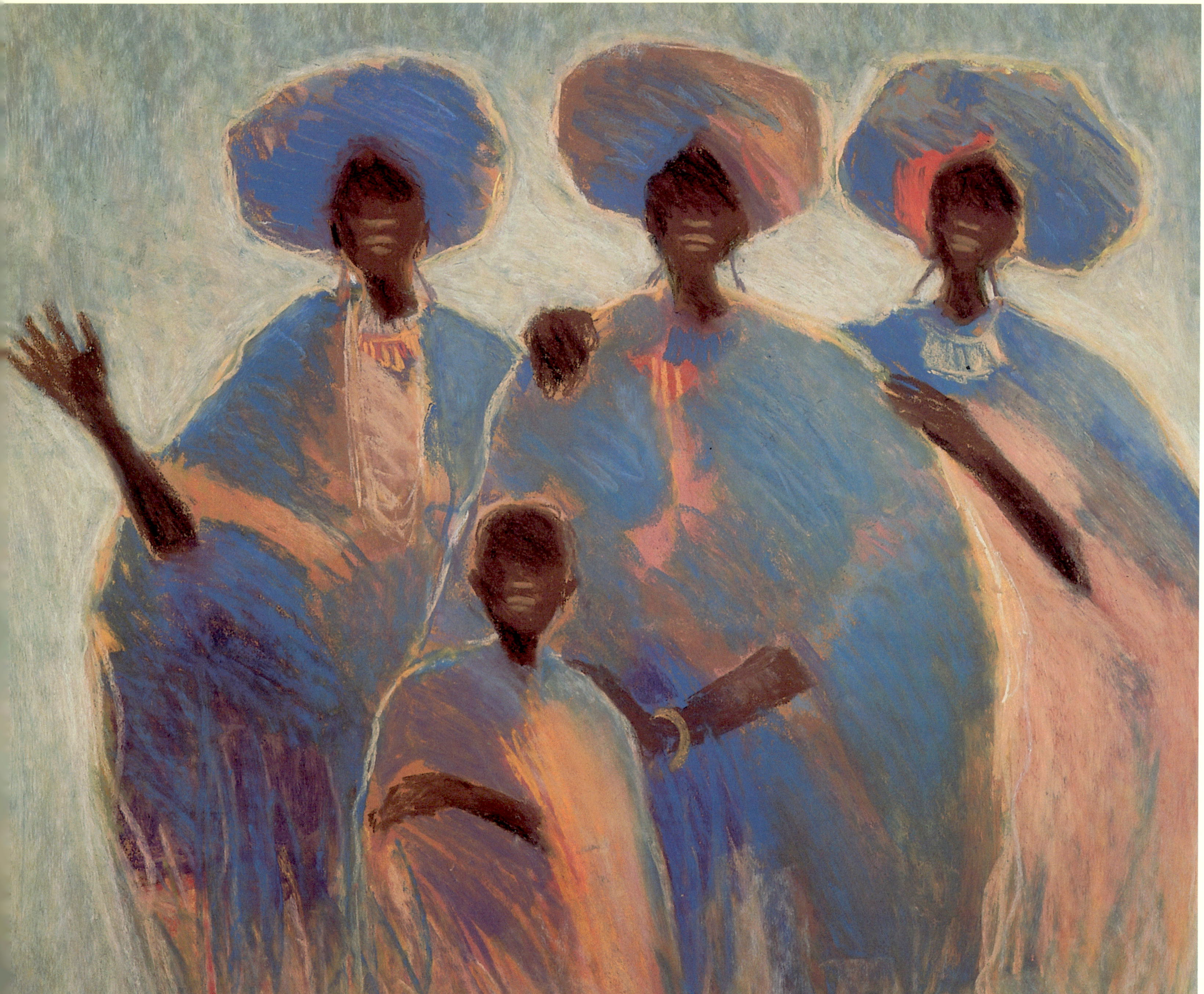

Unity *- The Tembu women learn to stick together and fend for themselves as the men have to work in the mines.*
(Pastel)

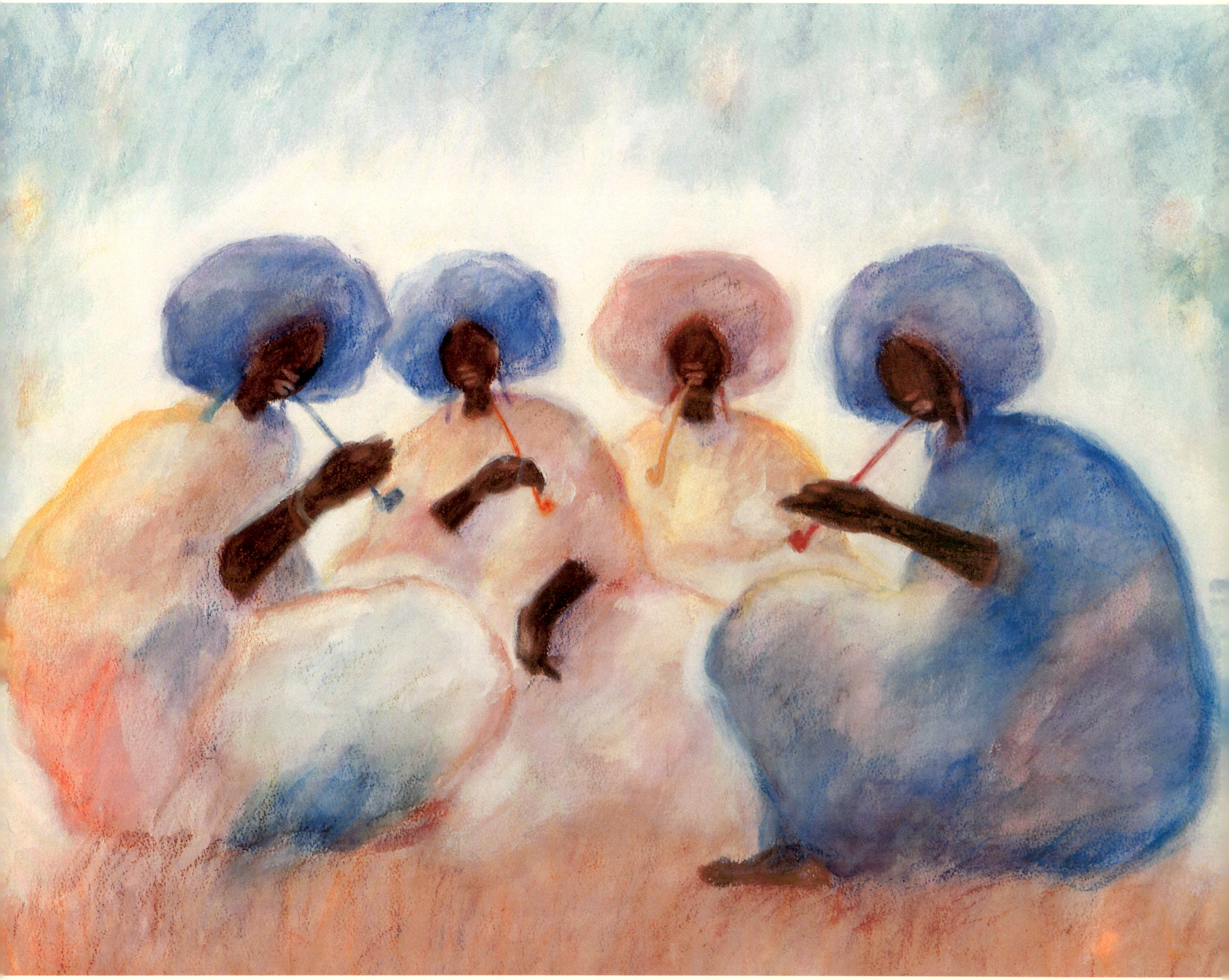

A Shared Smoke - *The Tembu enjoy the companionship of a sociable smoke. Using thin white clay pipes which they fashion themselves, they gossip and relax at the end of a day.*
(Pastel)

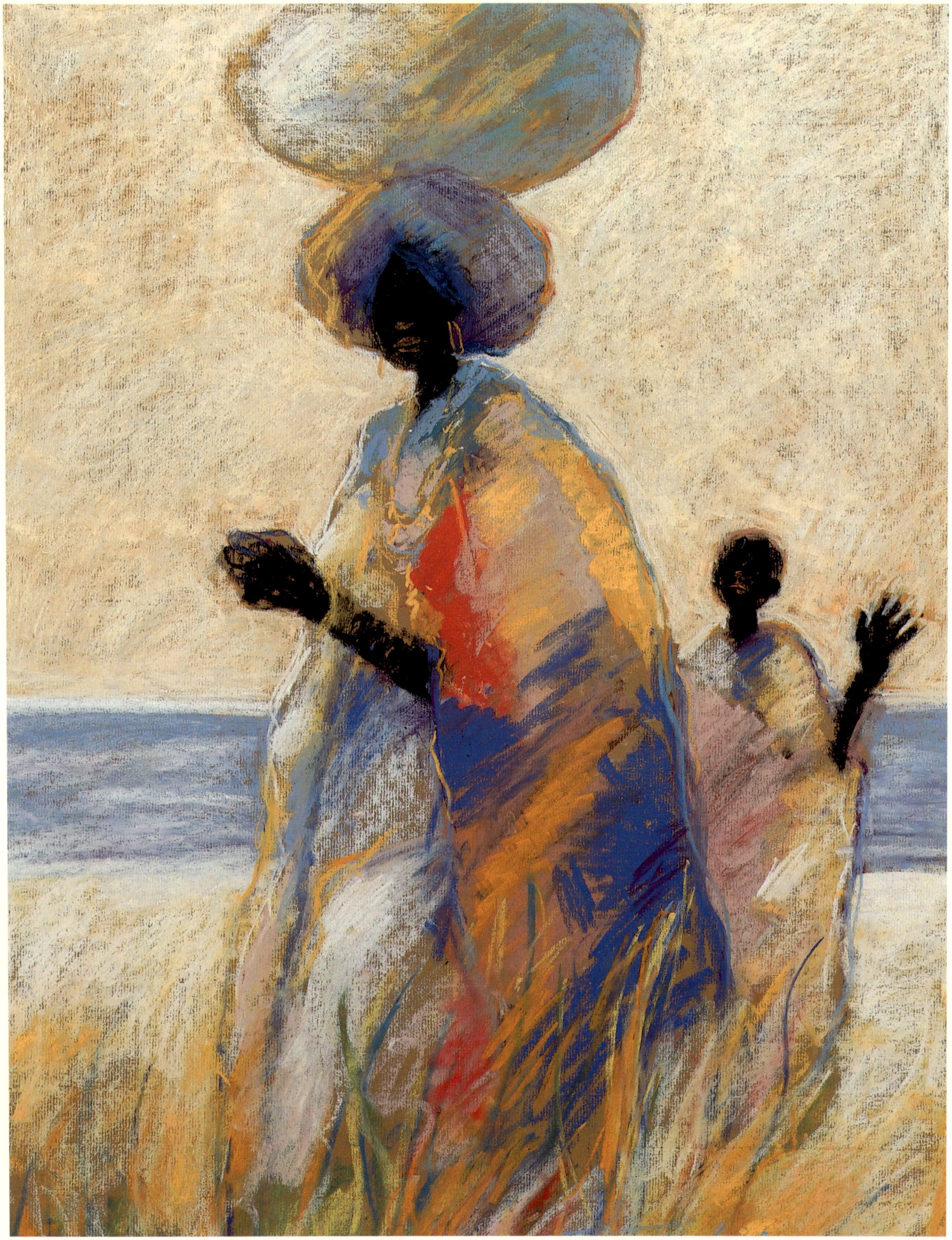

Tembu Woman & Child on Beach -
Open skies and the endless ocean give a feeling of space and eternity.
(Pastel)

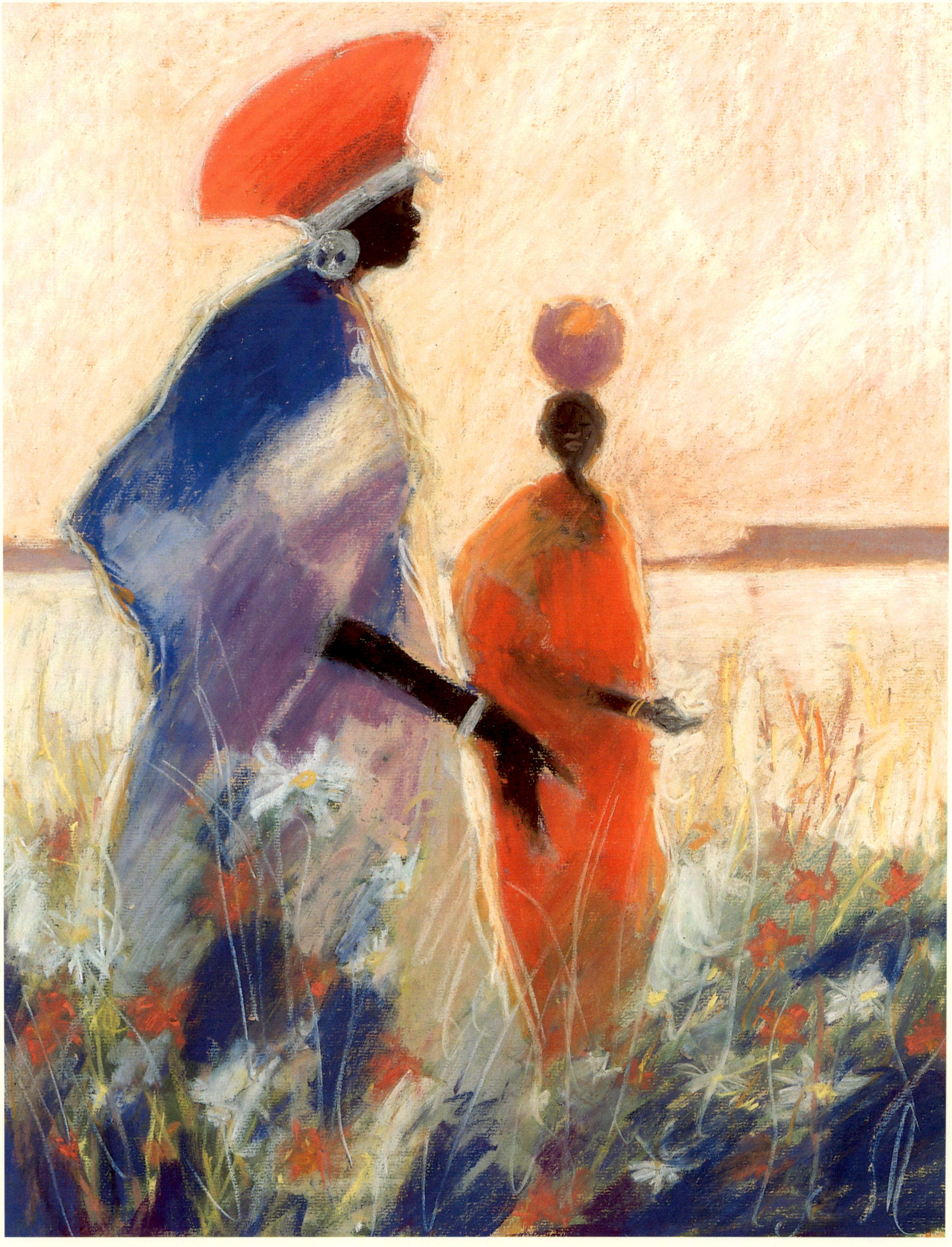

Mother & Child in Southern Africa -
At Easter time the fields are filled with beautiful cosmos flowers which bring colour to the landscape and joy to the people. (Pastel)

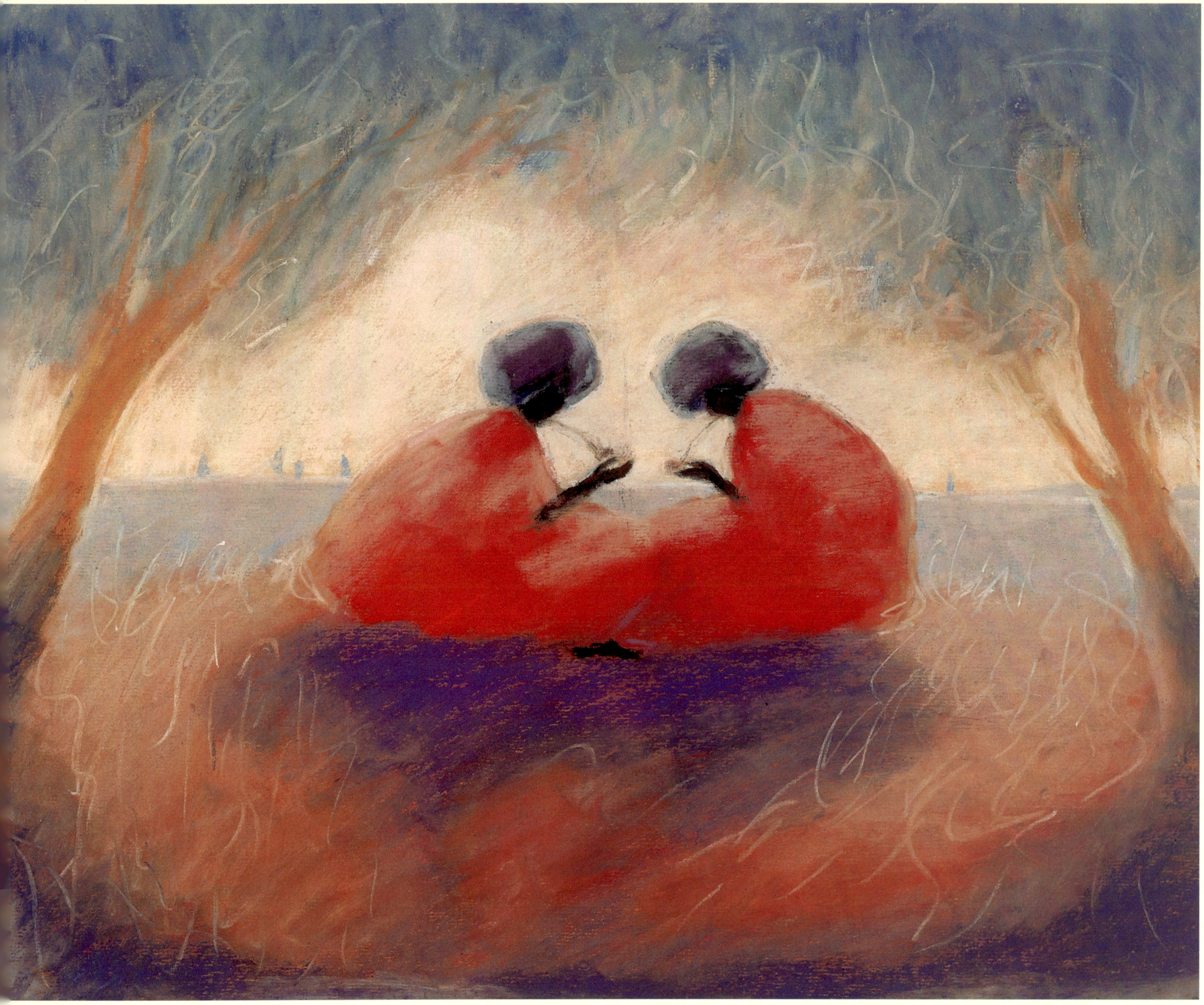

The Smokers - *The smoking of a traditional clay pipe is one of life's pleasures at the end of the day when troubles and joys can be shared with a friend.*
(Pastel)

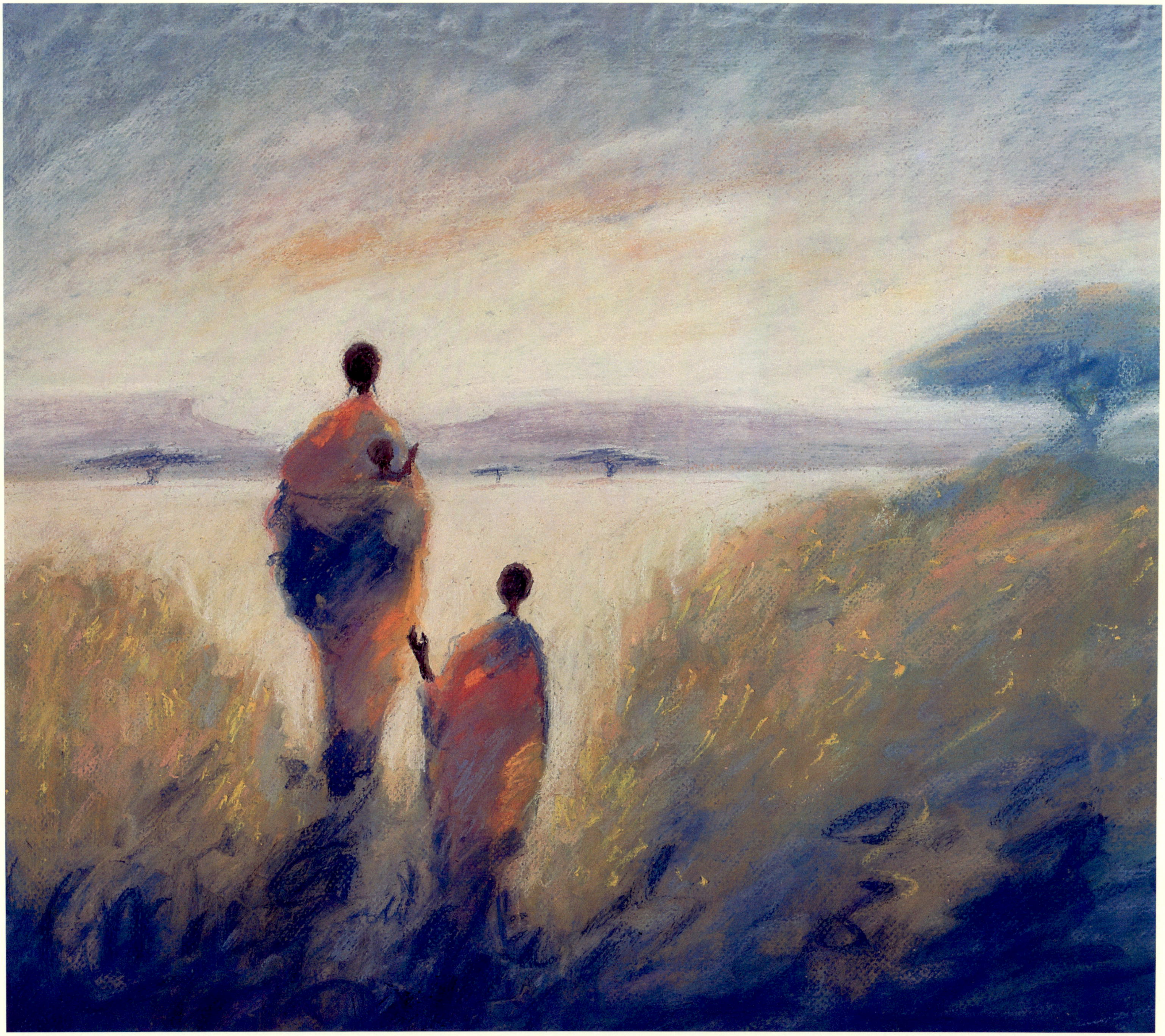

Emerging - *Africa is the cradle of mankind. From the earliest times, man has awoken beneath the warm rays of the sun, ready to face the challenges which lie ahead. (Pastel)*

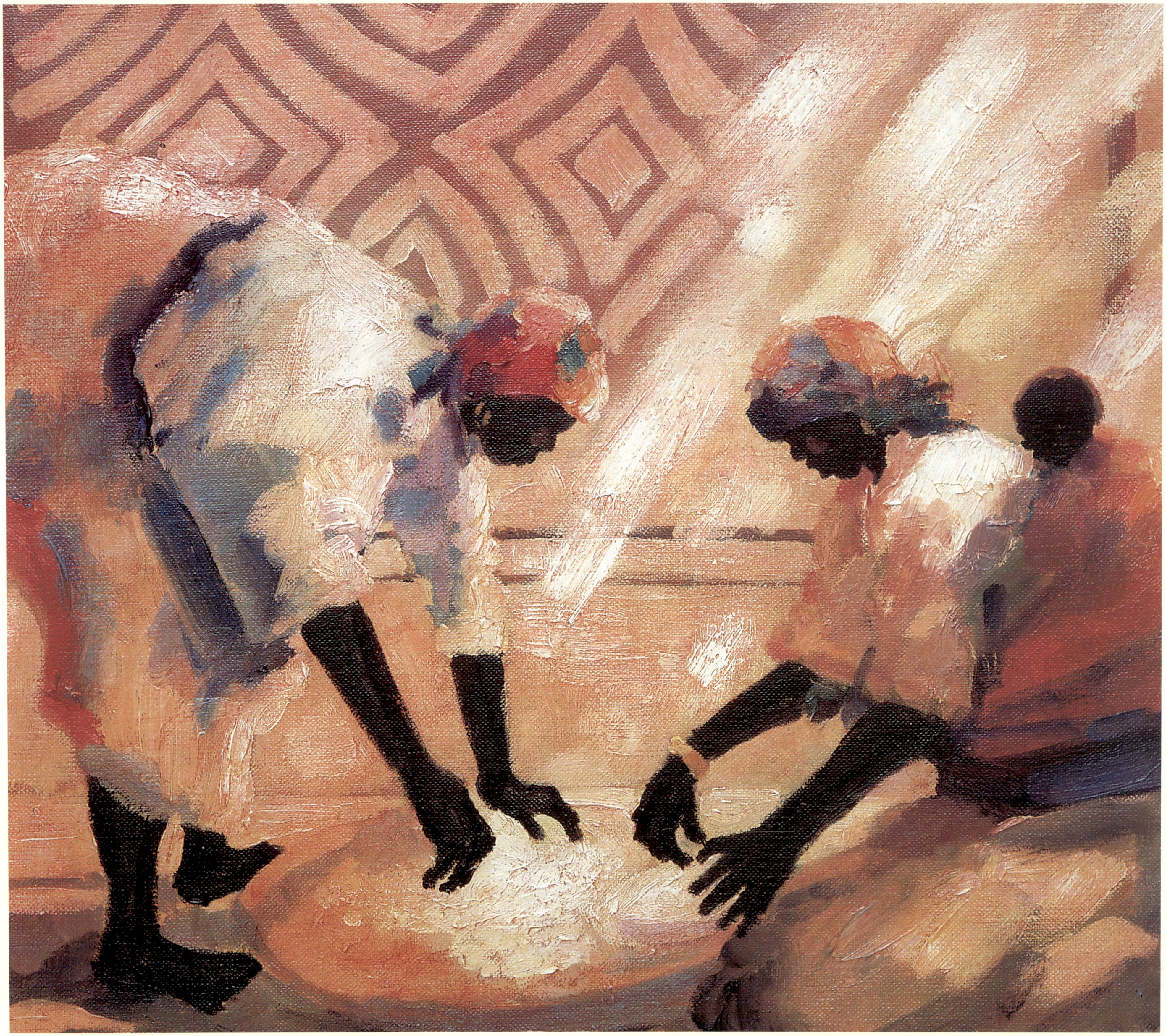

Women Making Mealie - *The hands of African women are never still. Women create the litema design on the hut in the background with mud, dung and stones, while those in the foreground are hard at work grinding corn into mealie flour which is the staple diet for many. (Acrylic)*

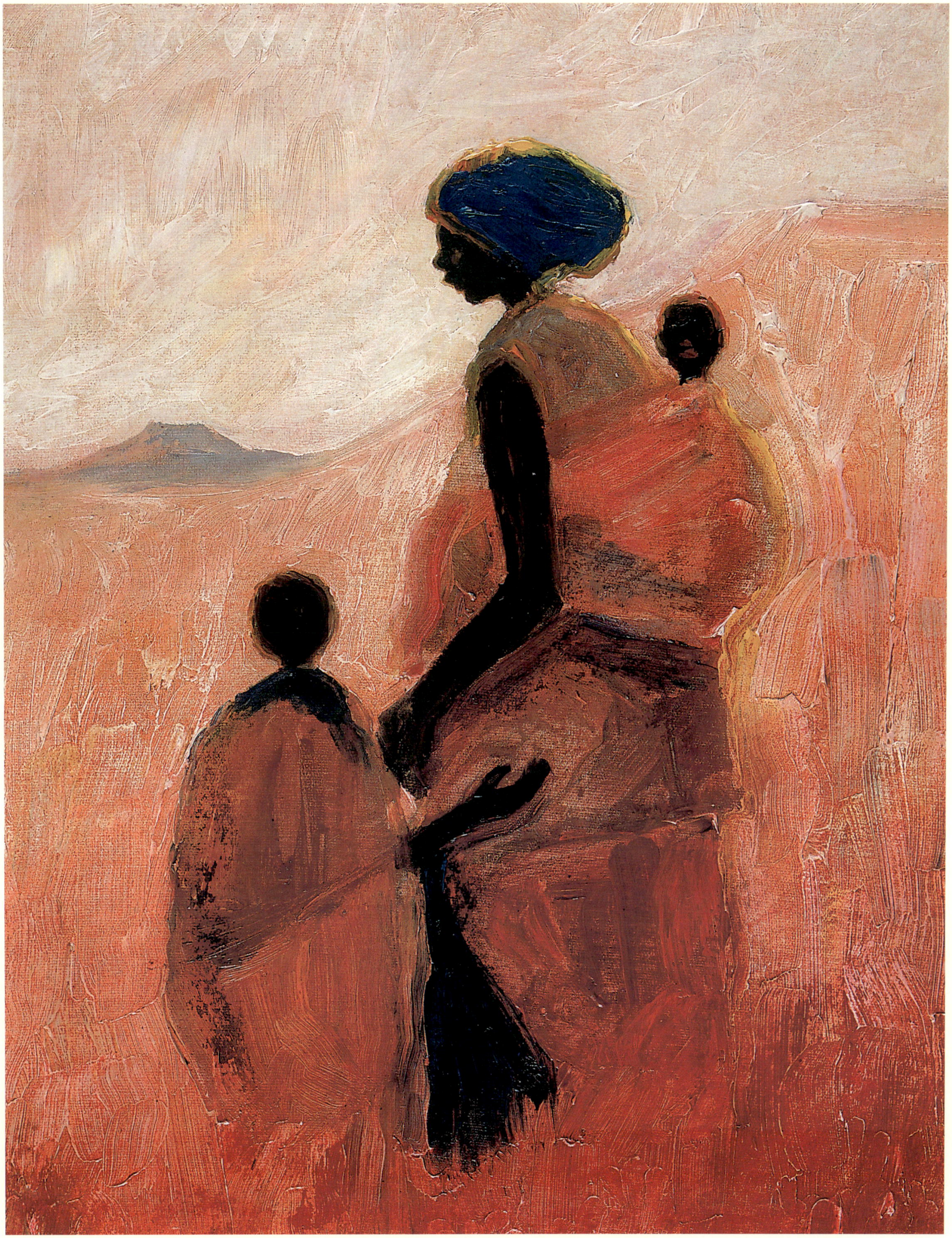

Mother and Children - *The African woman nurtures both the land and the children of this vast continent. Strong bonds tie her to the family, just as her baby is tightly bonded to her working back. (Acrylic)*

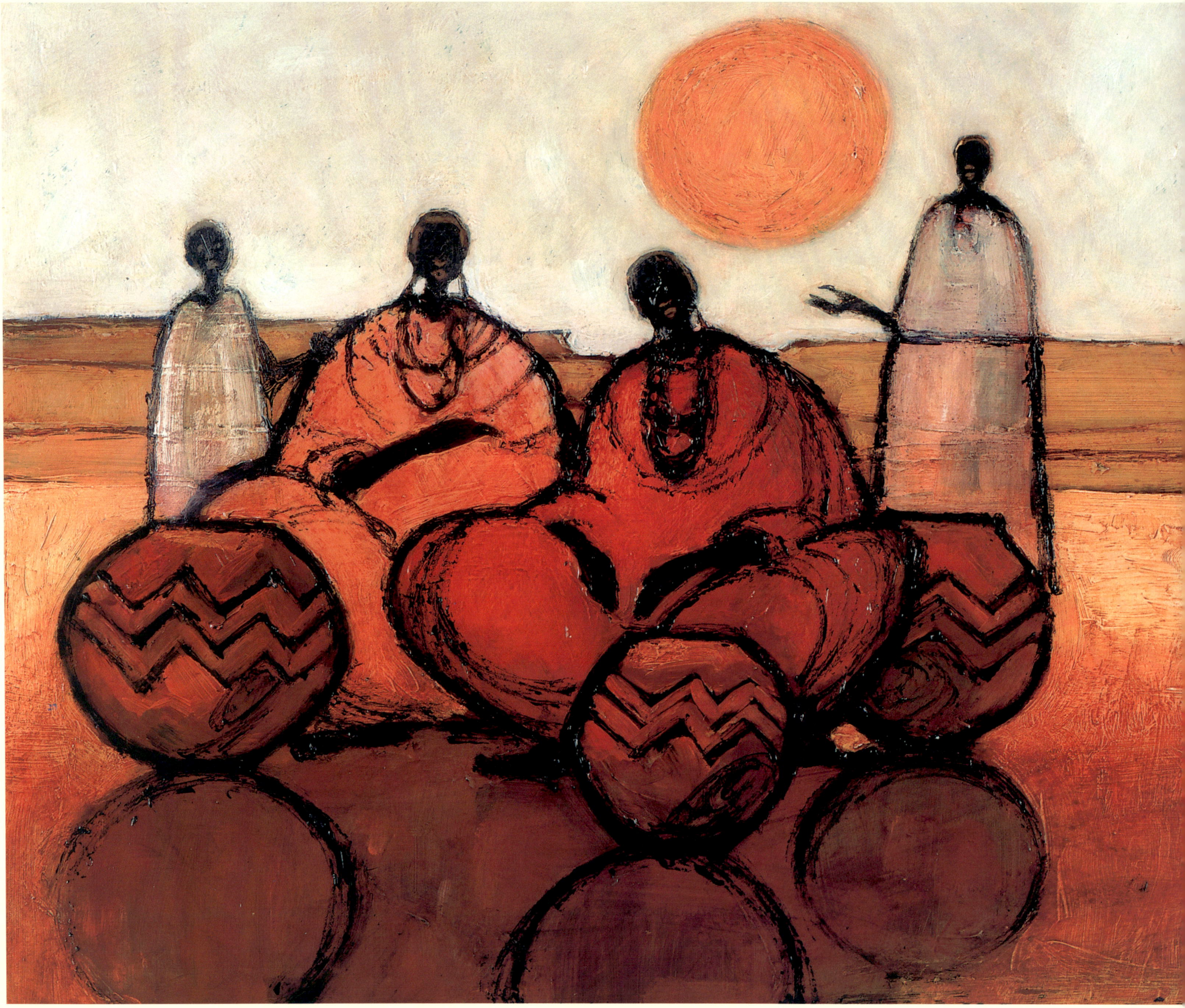

The Circles of Life - *A favourite theme of Tony's. The roundness of the moon, the symmetrical pots and the fertile women of Africa symbolise the continuous cycle of humanity. Life in Africa is dependent on women and water.*
(Acrylic)

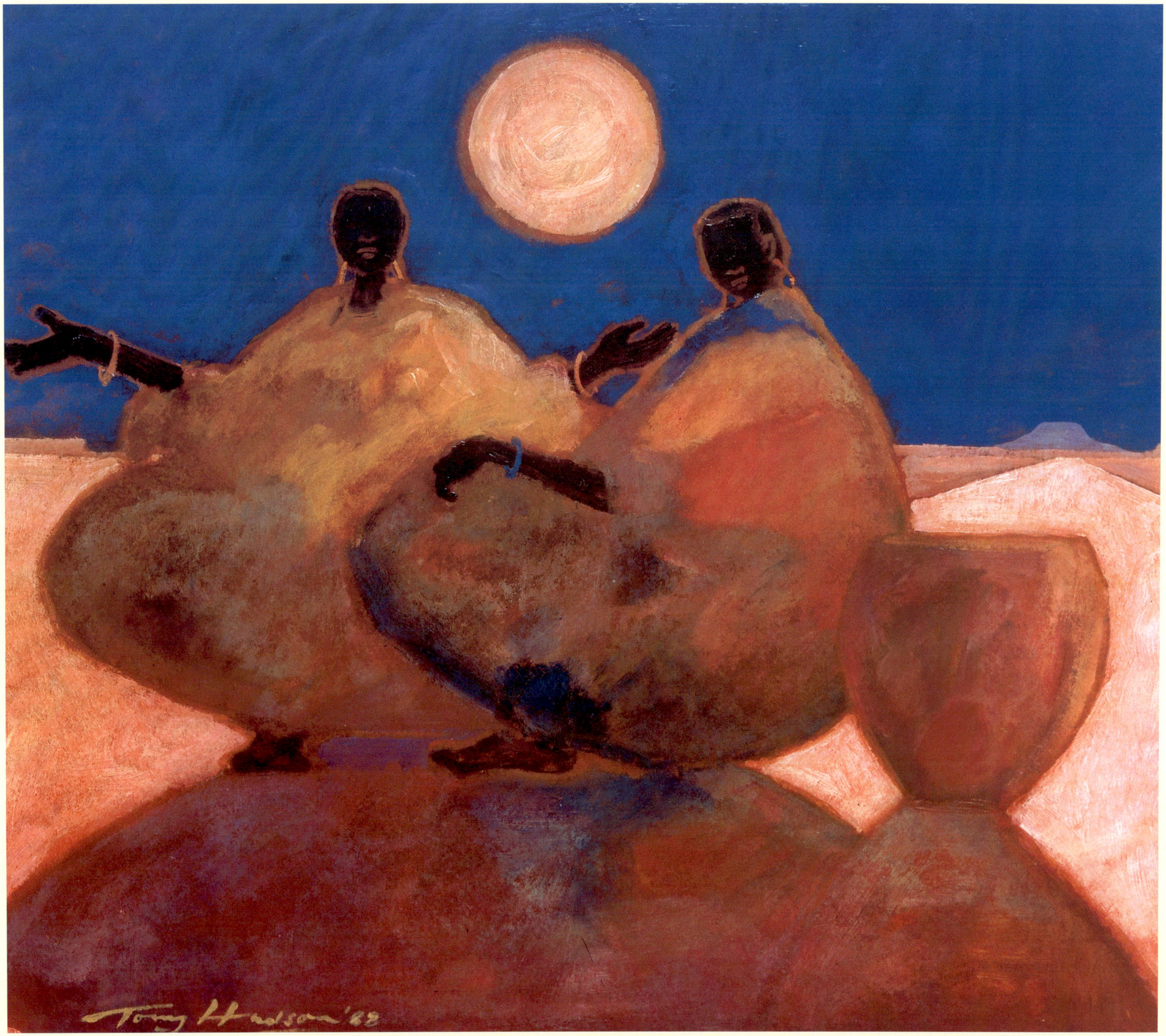

The Water Cycle - *While the Moon's cycle affects the tides, the women's cycle ensures that the life in their bodies and the water in their pots are constantly renewed. (Acrylic)*

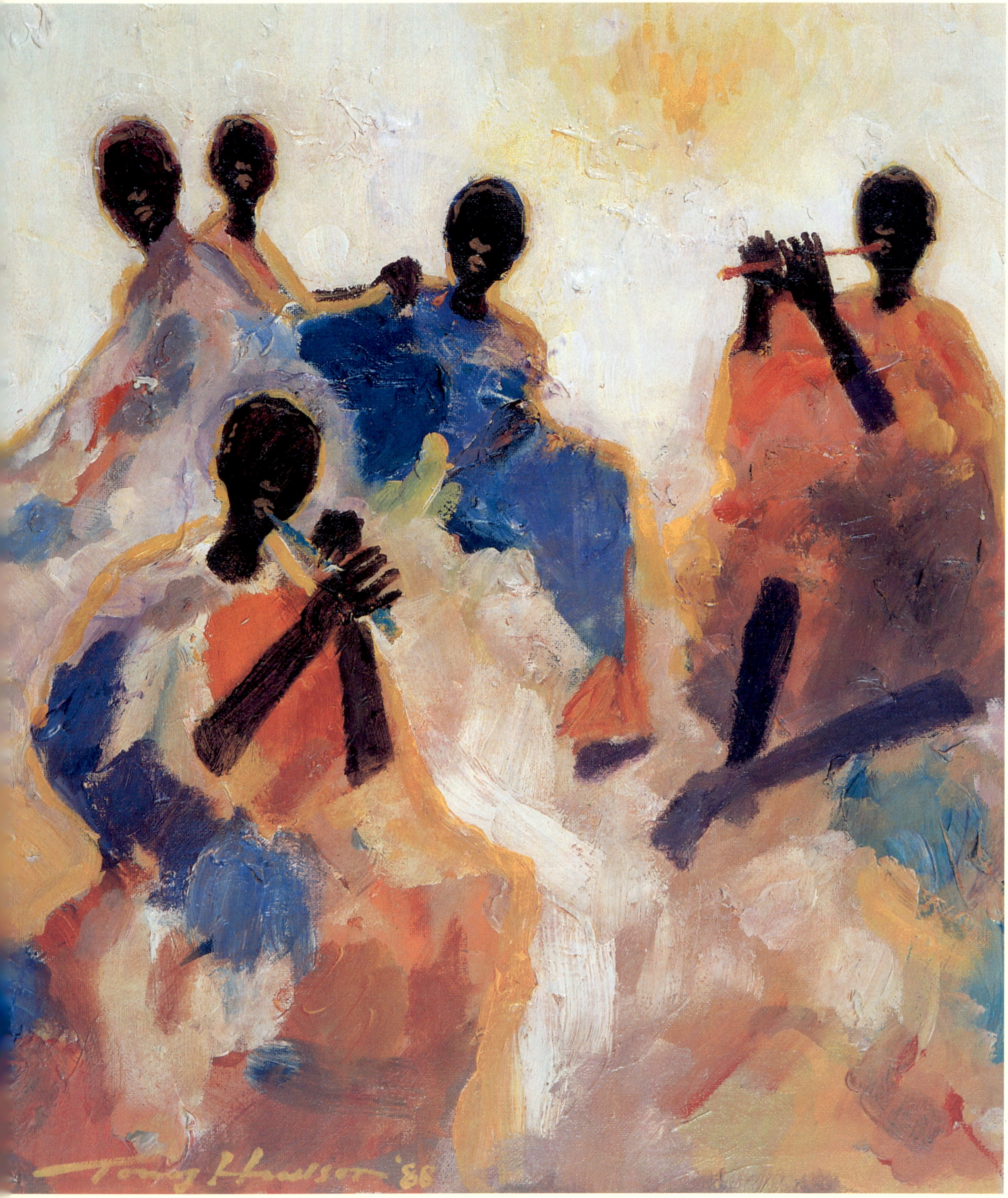

The Players - *Music is at the heart of African celebrations. African music has influenced musicians across the world with its rhythm and power drawn from the simplest of instruments. (Acrylic)*

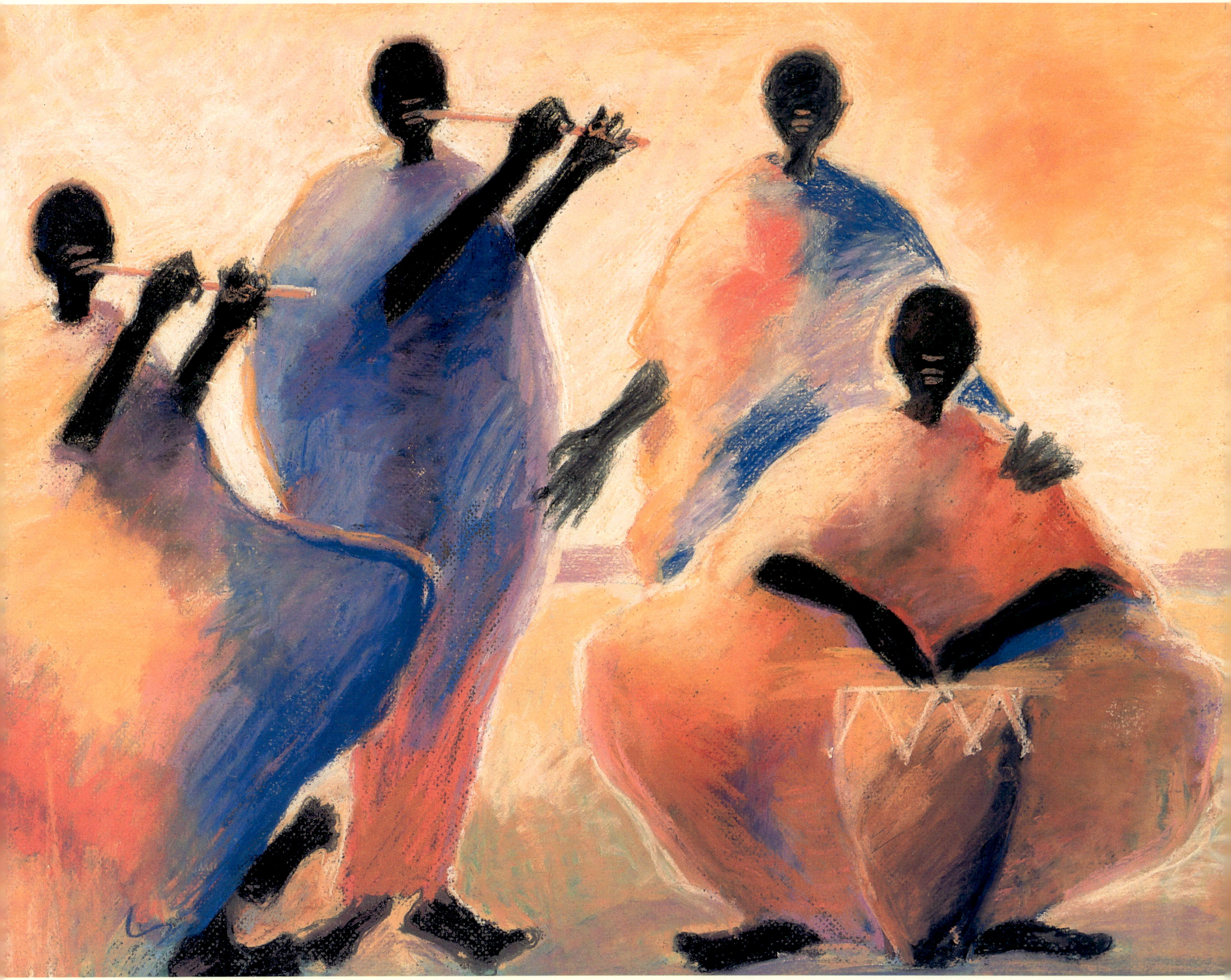

In Harmony *- Music is a fundamental part of any culture. In Lesotho the men play the instruments while the women sing.*
(Pastel)

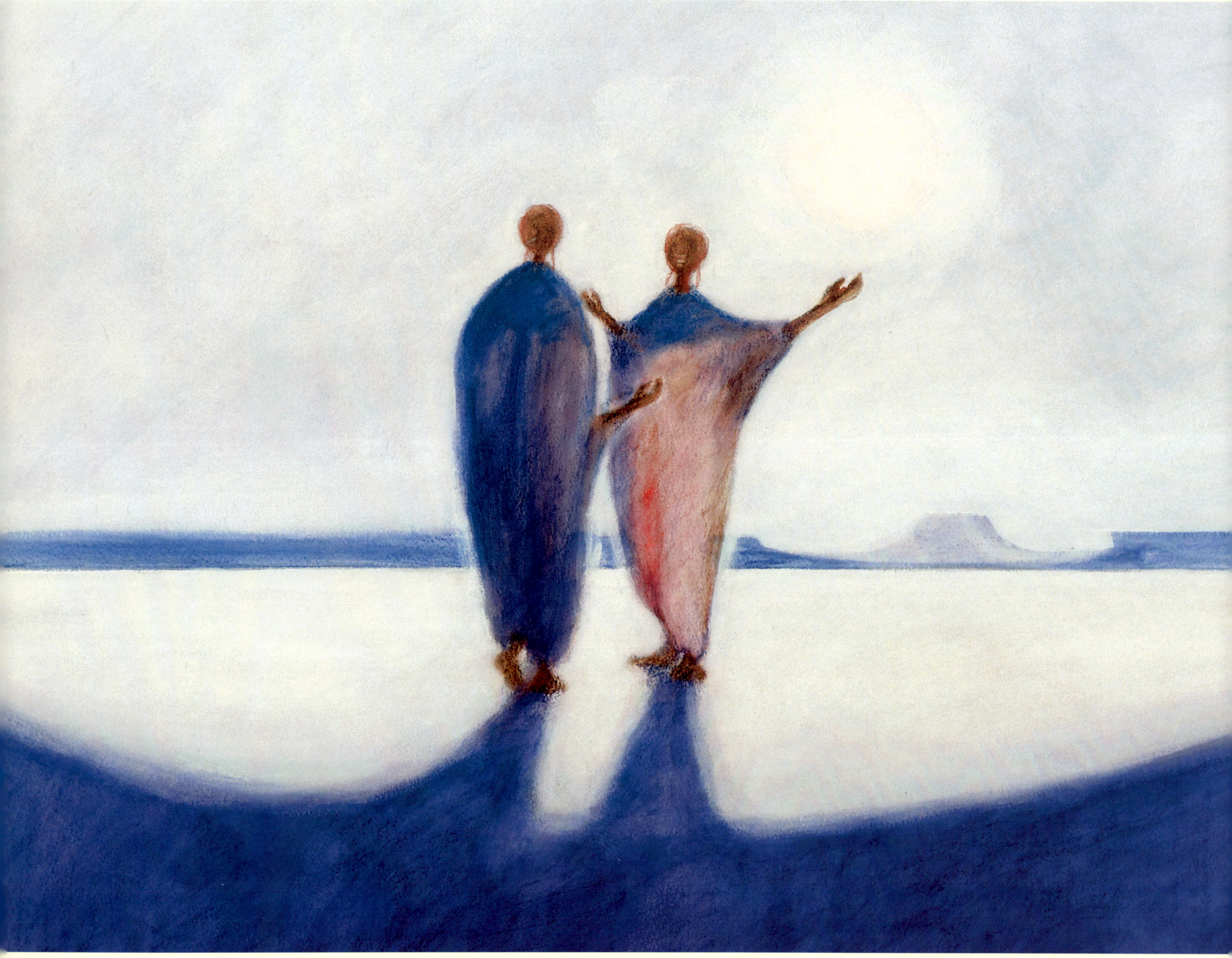

My Friend **-** *As their shadows echo the ageless mountains beyond, two friends greet each other. Friendship as enduring as the hills makes life less lonely and brings warmth to the soul.*
(Pastel & Watercolour)

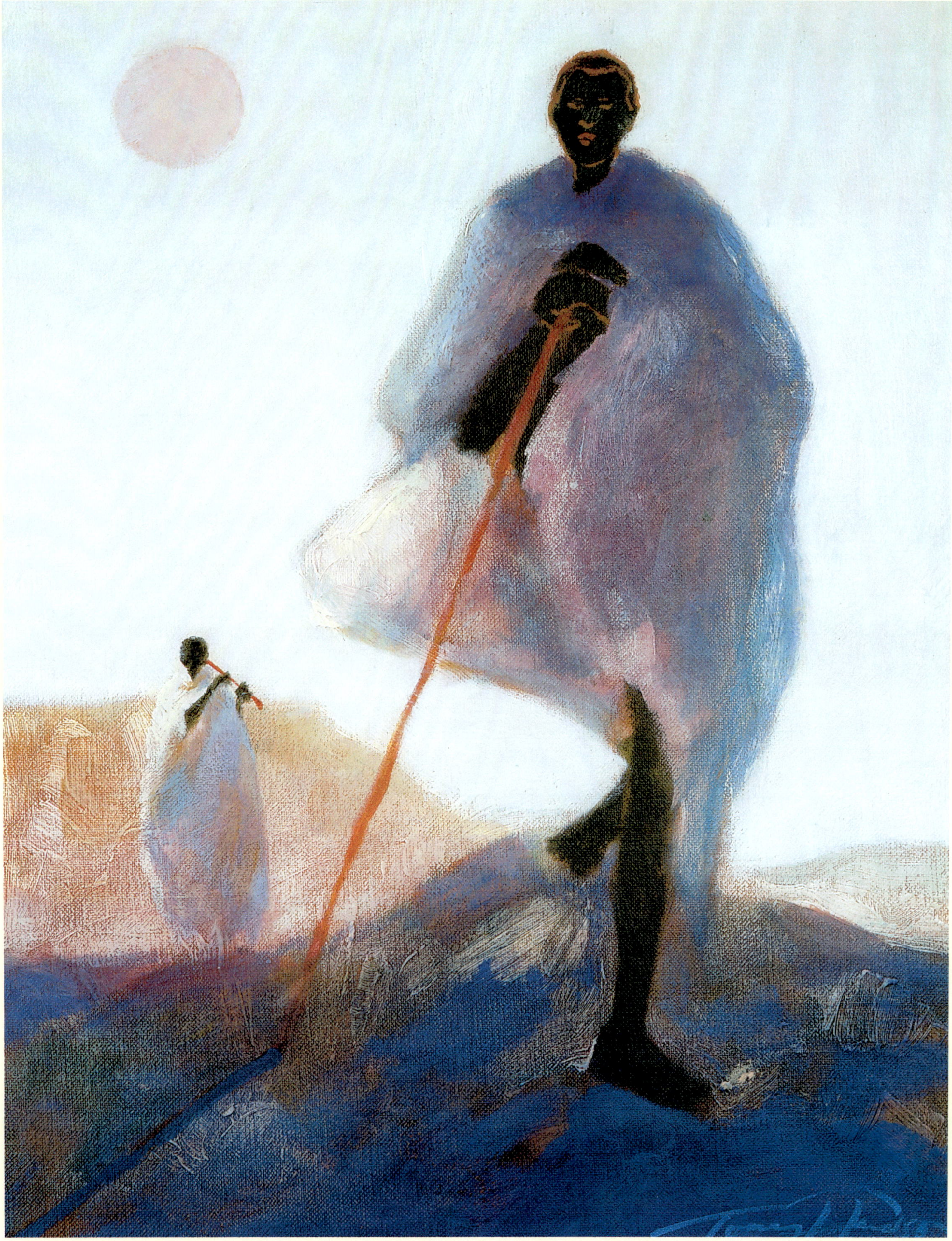

Contemplation - *The mysteries and traditions of Africa go back to the beginning of time. This is truly a country where one should stop and stare in order to take in the vastness of the landscape. (Pastel)*

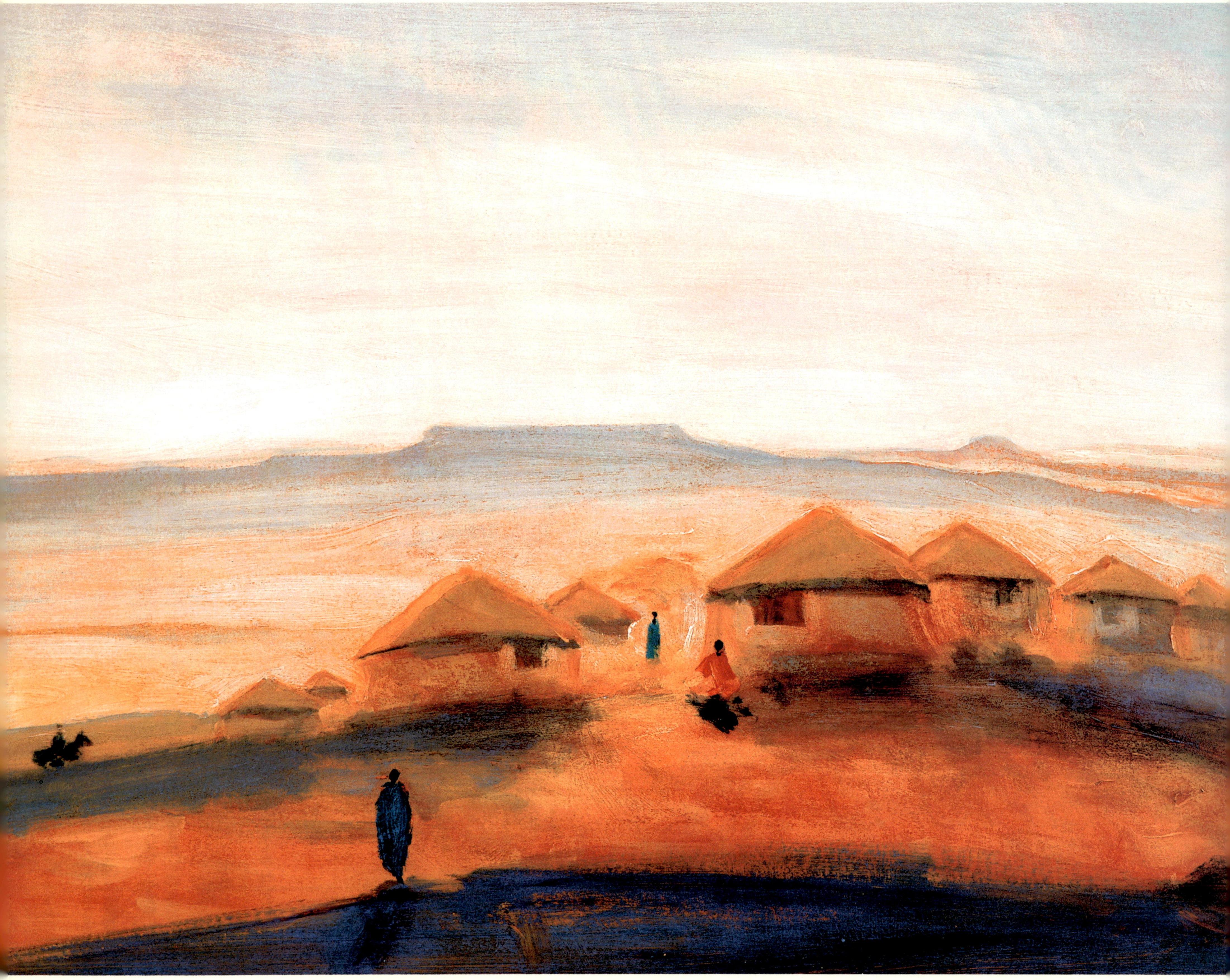

The Village *- A typical Basotho village consists of several round houses known as 'Rondavels'*
(Acrylic)

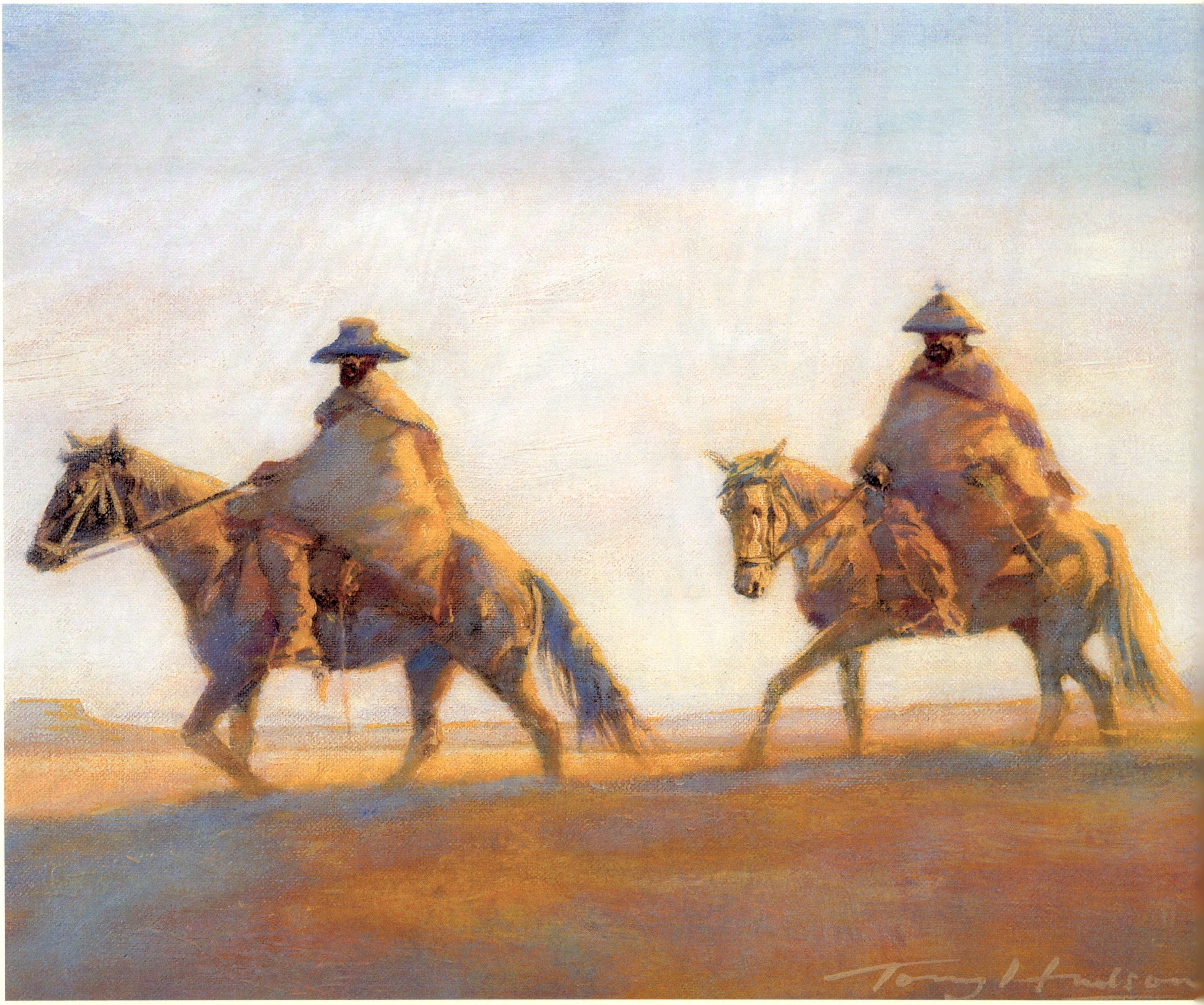

Sunrise *- Golden rays of sunshine cast a warm glow over the blanketed figures of these isolated horsemen as they set off across the cold and barren landscape. (Acrylic)*

Landscapes of Africa

At sunrise and sunset the mountains take on mystical colours and shapes. At certain times the mountains seem hard and clear as they recede into the distance: a fantastic series of brightly coloured cut-outs. At other times haze dissolves the edges and outlines, transforming the entire range into a fusion of pure colour. While travelling in the mountains Tony made a lot of sketches of the shapes of peaks and ridges and the curves of the valleys. The mountain pictures are painted from these sketches. To Tony the colours were completely unforgettable.

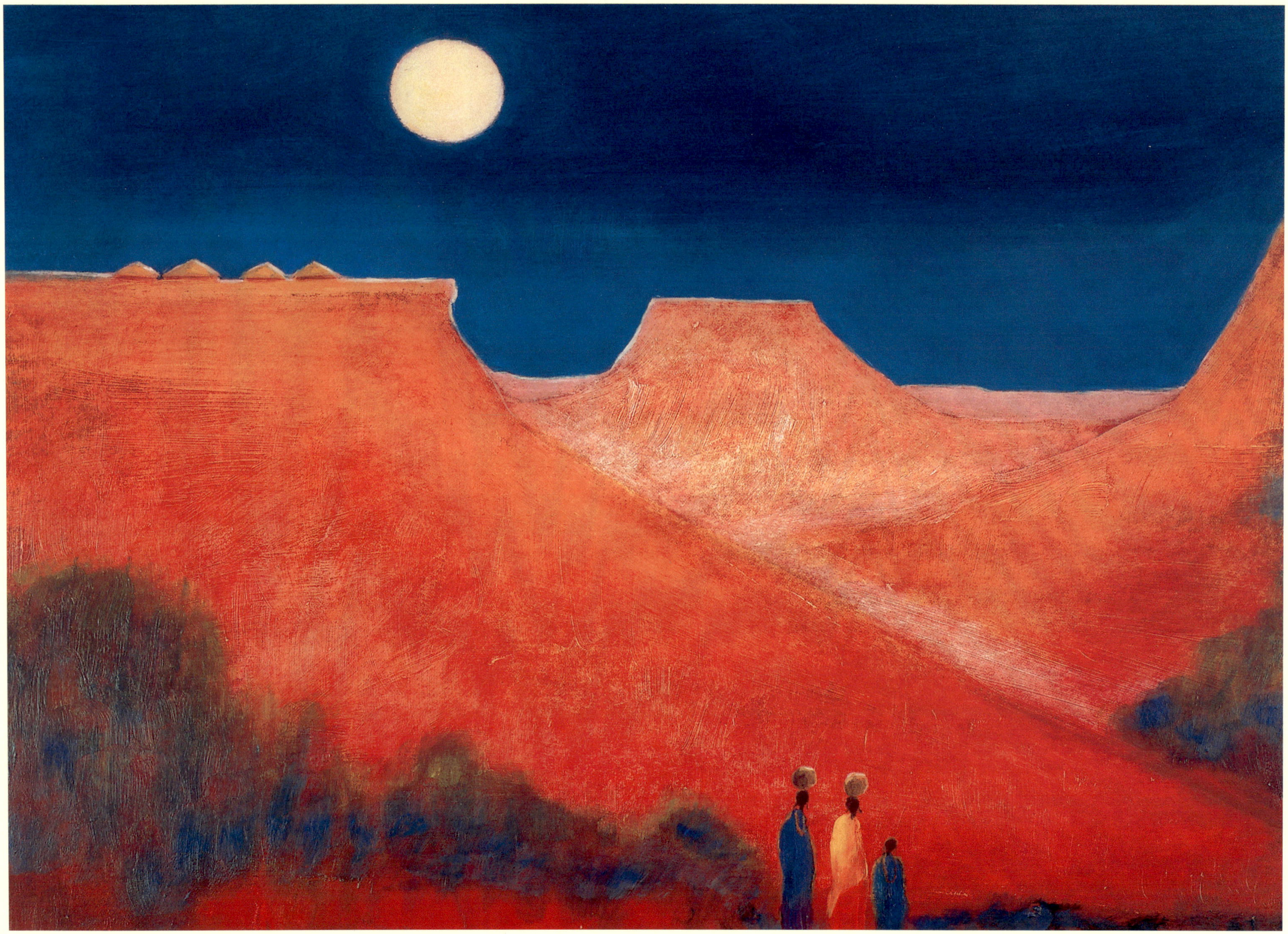

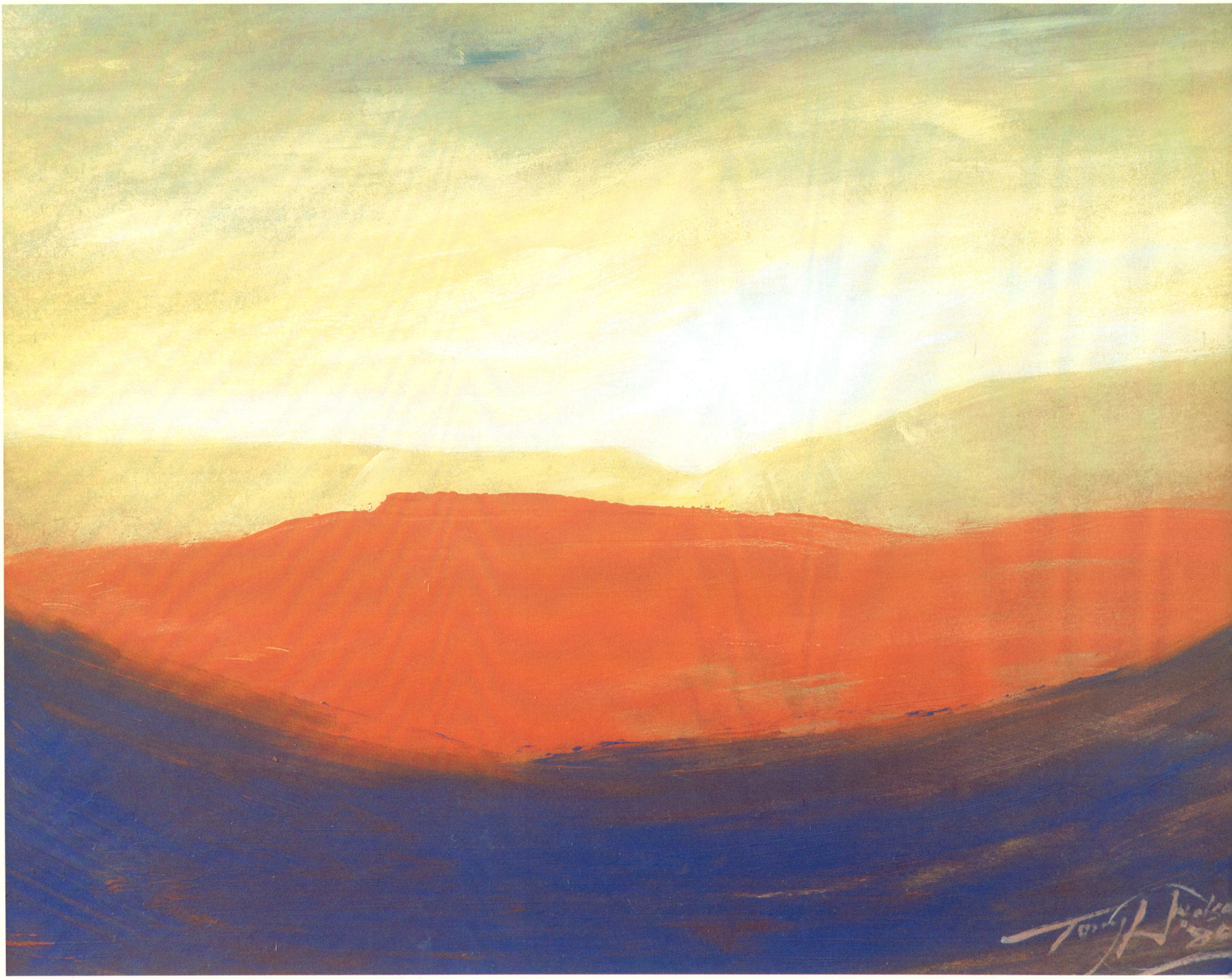

Horizons **-** *The ever-changing shades of the mountains stretch out into endless horizons. Such open perspectives allow the soul to soar and the heart to sing. (Acrylic)*

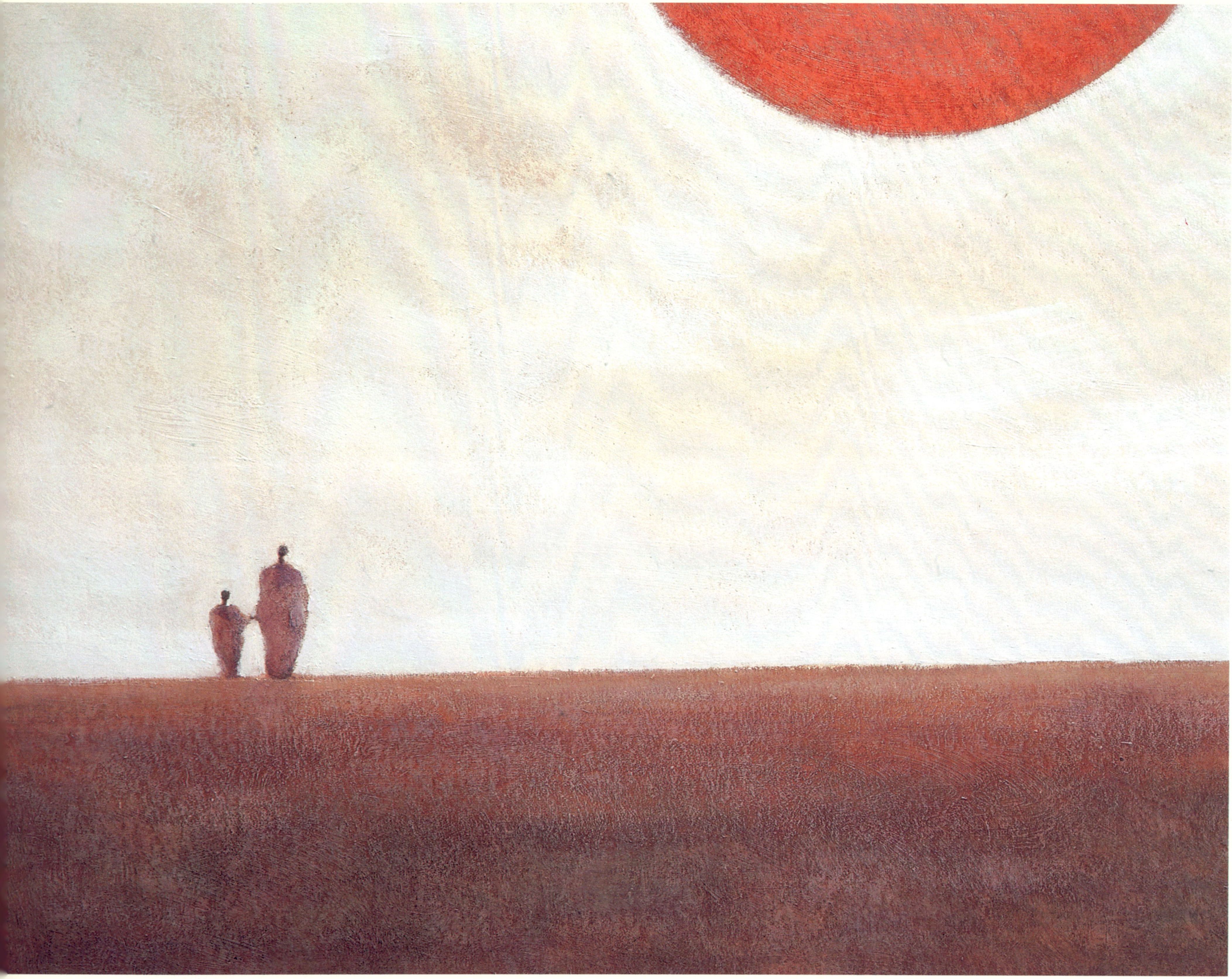

The Heat of the Day - *The scorching sun hangs over the heads of the walkers like a pendulum. One cannot survive for long under the heat of an African sun without shade or water.*
(Acrylic)

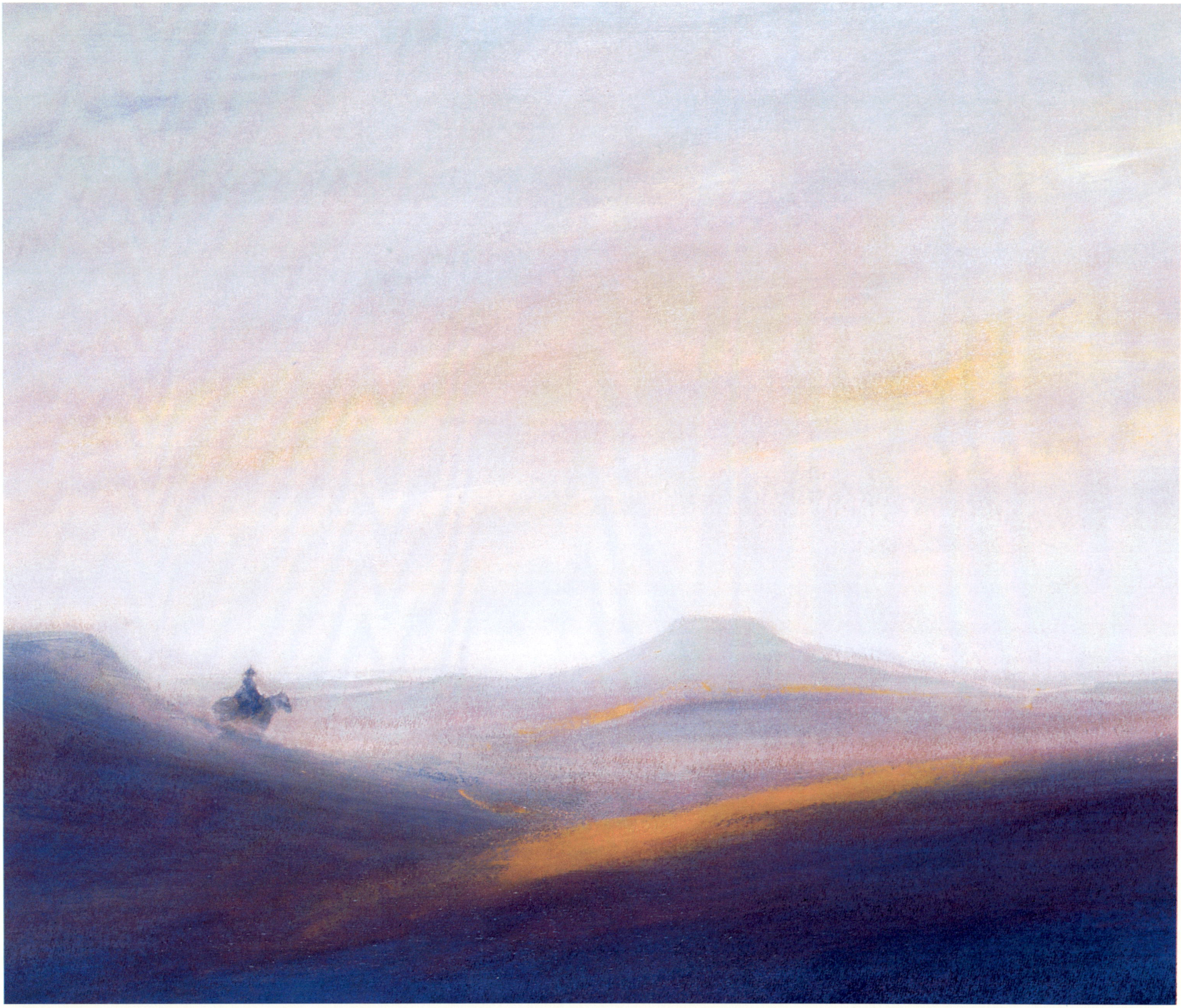

In The Blue - *Blue skies, blue mountain ranges and clear blue streams of mountain water mirror the clarity of the atmosphere at the top of this mountain kingdom. (Acrylic)*

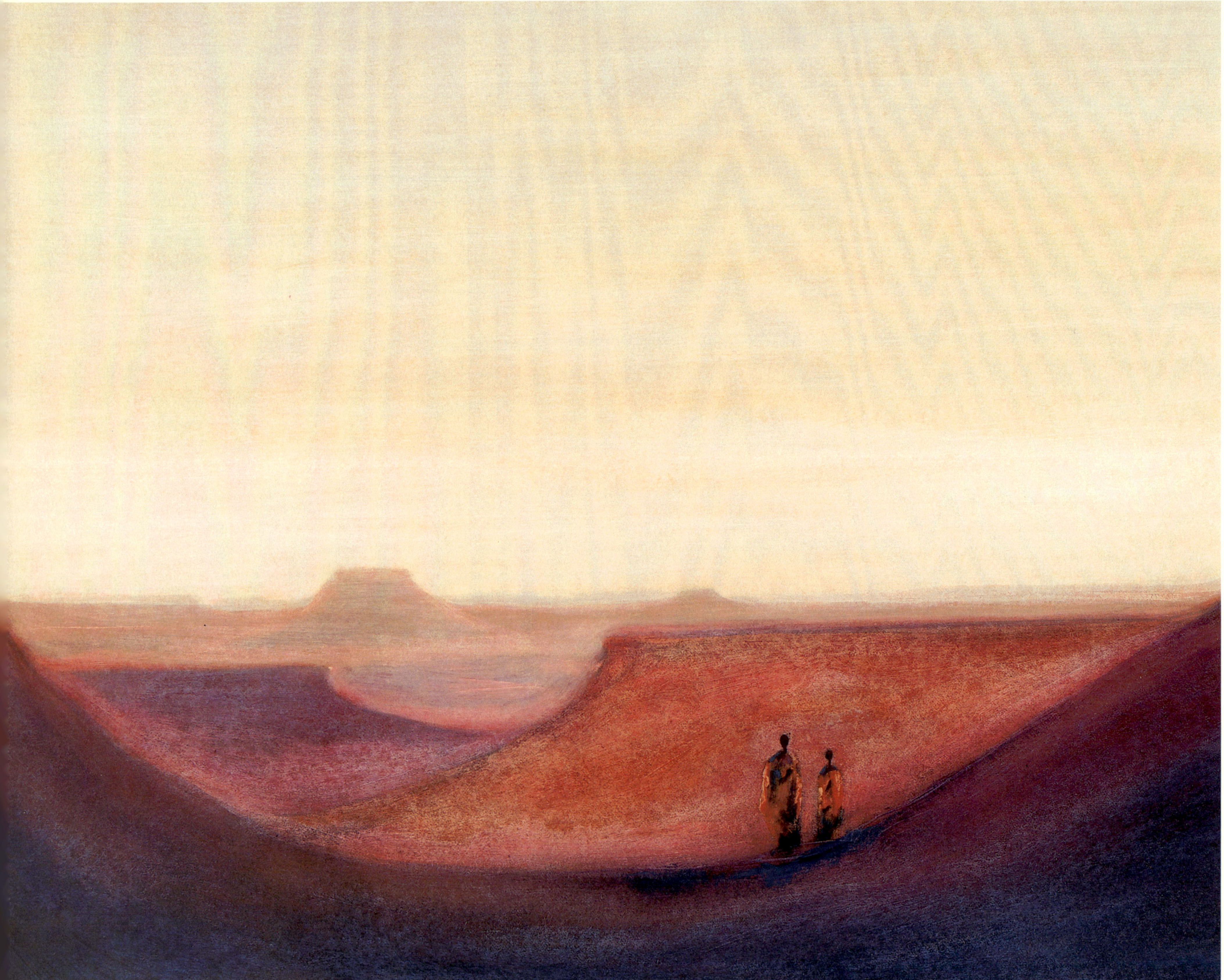

***The Journey** - Distances are vast and roads are scarce in many parts of Africa. Without water and shade the journey can be hazardous and not all survive the harshness of the land or its elements.*
(Acrylic)

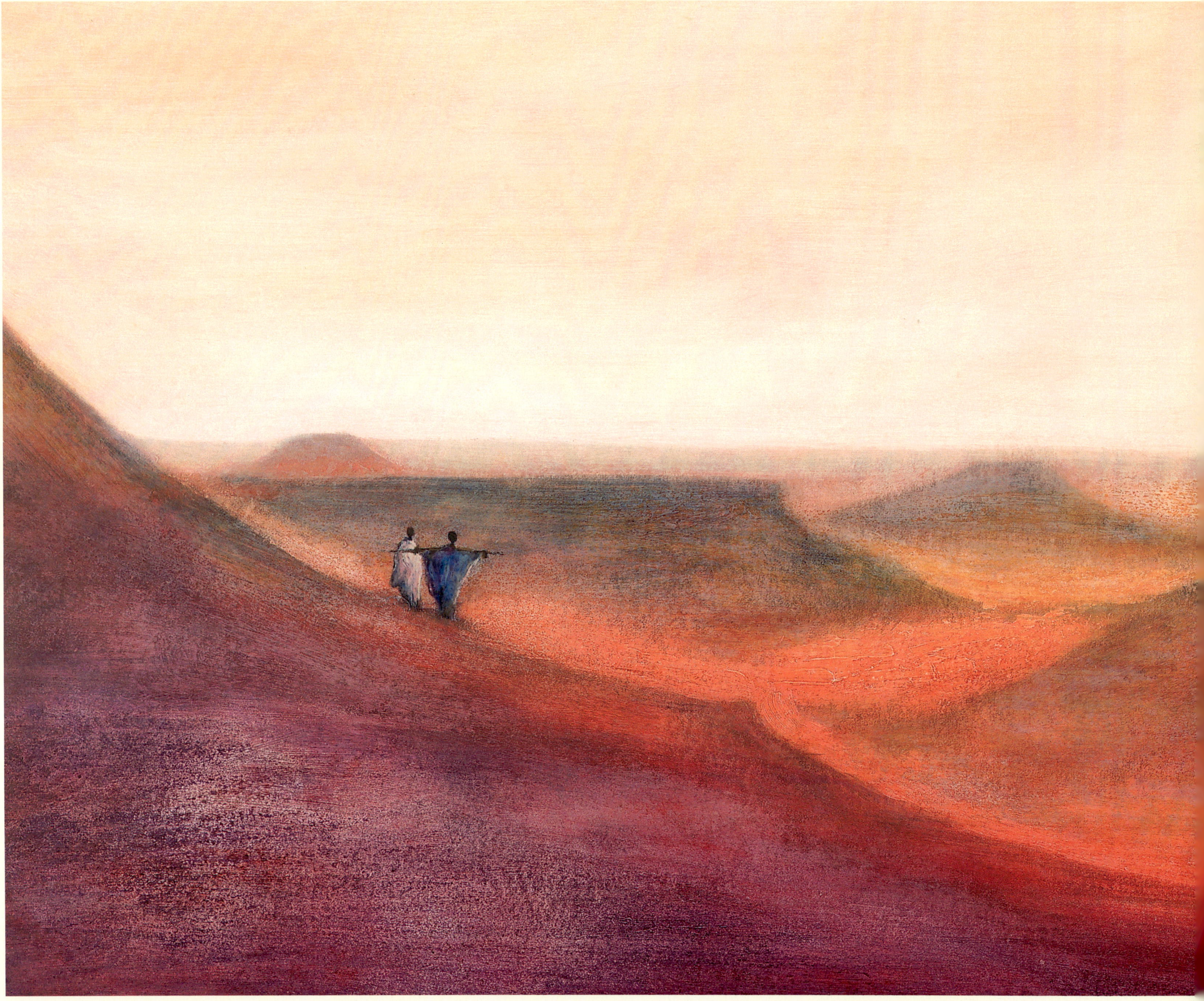

Our Land - *This almost biblical view emphasises man's insignificance in the vast lands of Africa as the mountains stretch out to a distant horizon.*
(Acrylic)

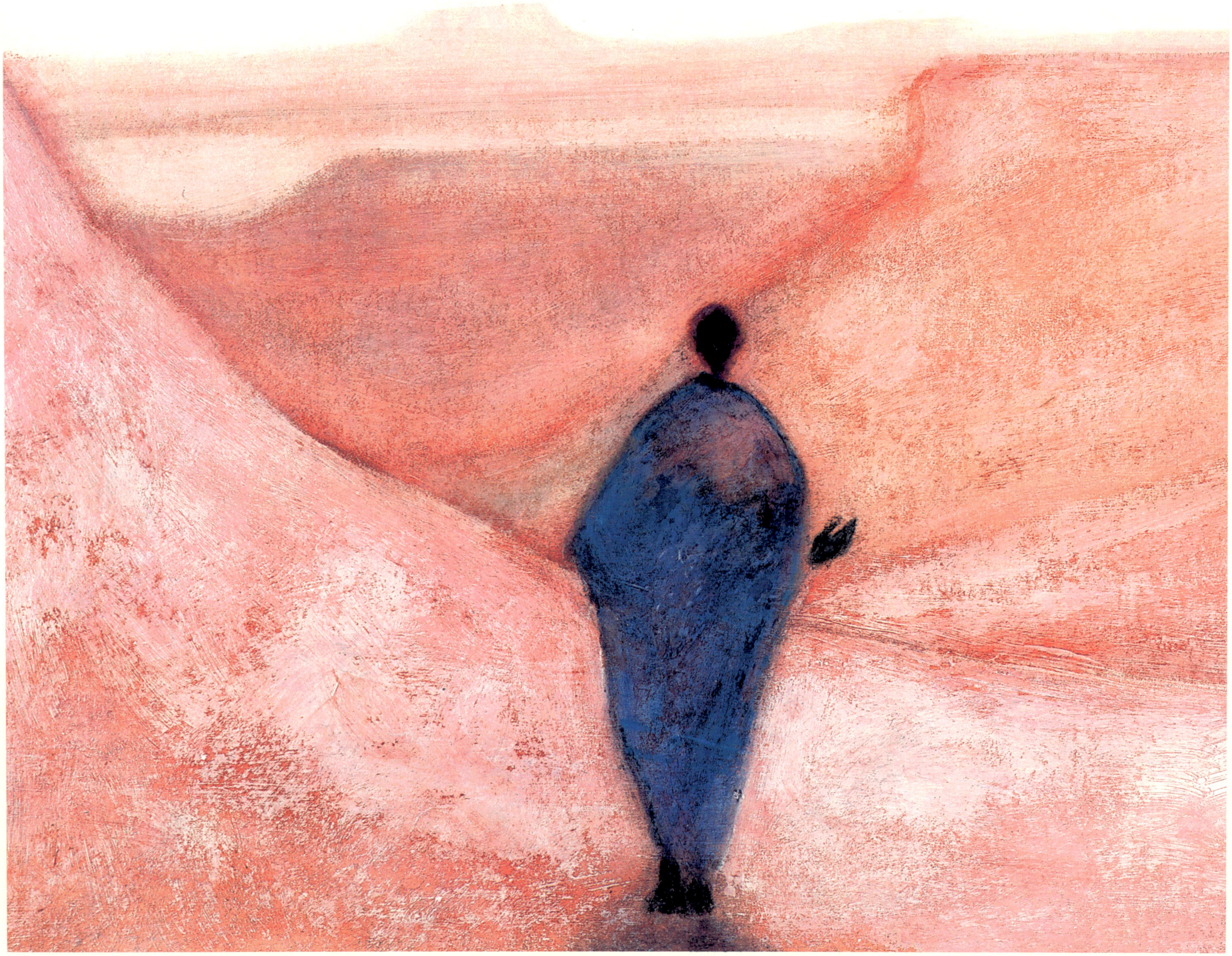

Solitary **-** *Alone, but at one with his environment, the blanketed figure seeks his destiny on the other side of the mountain range.*
(Acrylic)

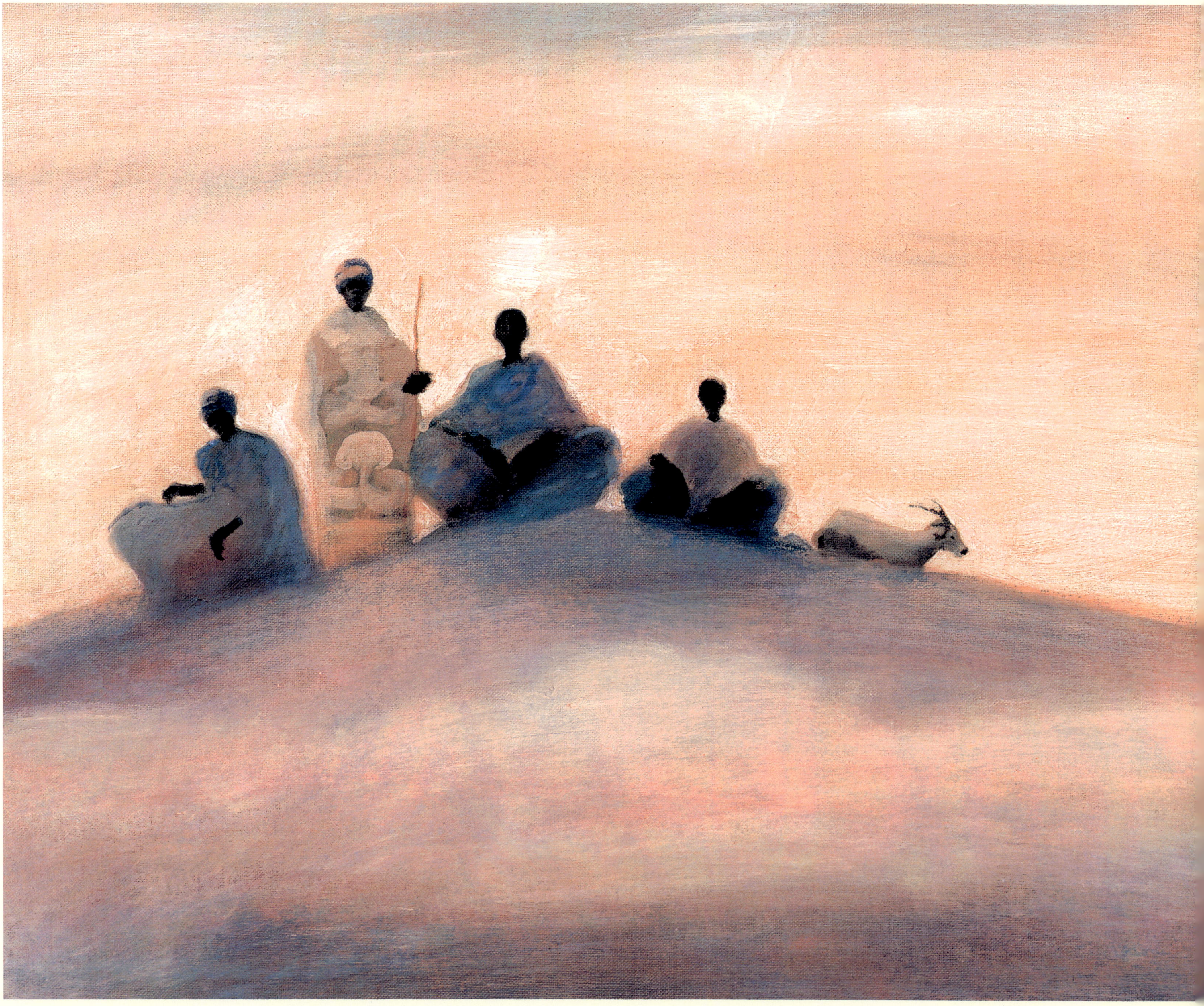

Community *- Young and unschooled, these herdboys are nonetheless wise in the ways of the mountains and of the animals in their care. Often cold and afraid, they need the company of their friends to ward off loneliness.*
(Acrylic)

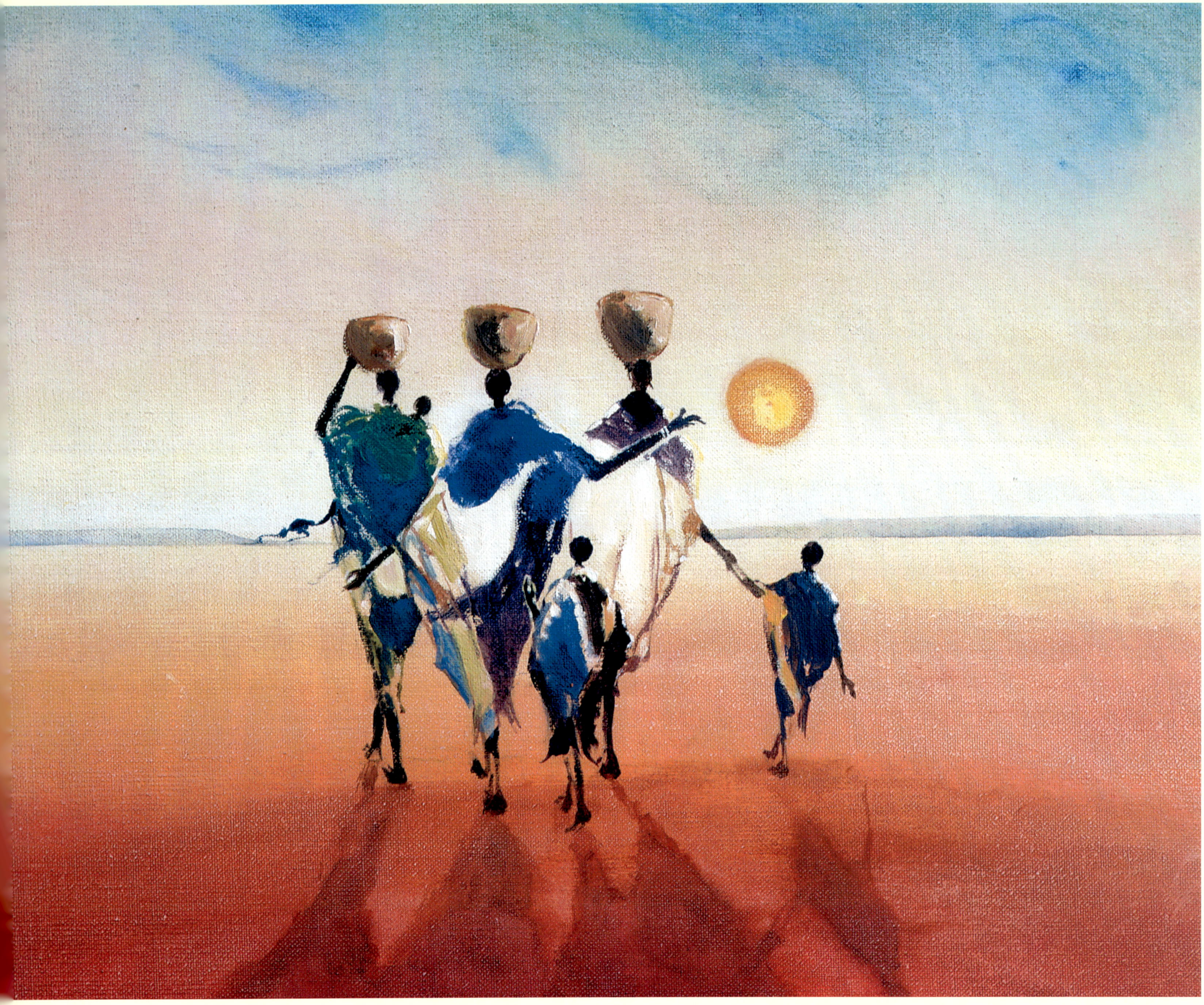

Going Home **-** *Life in Africa begins with sunrise. When the sun begins to set, the day's work is done and it is time to return to the security of home.*
(Acrylic)

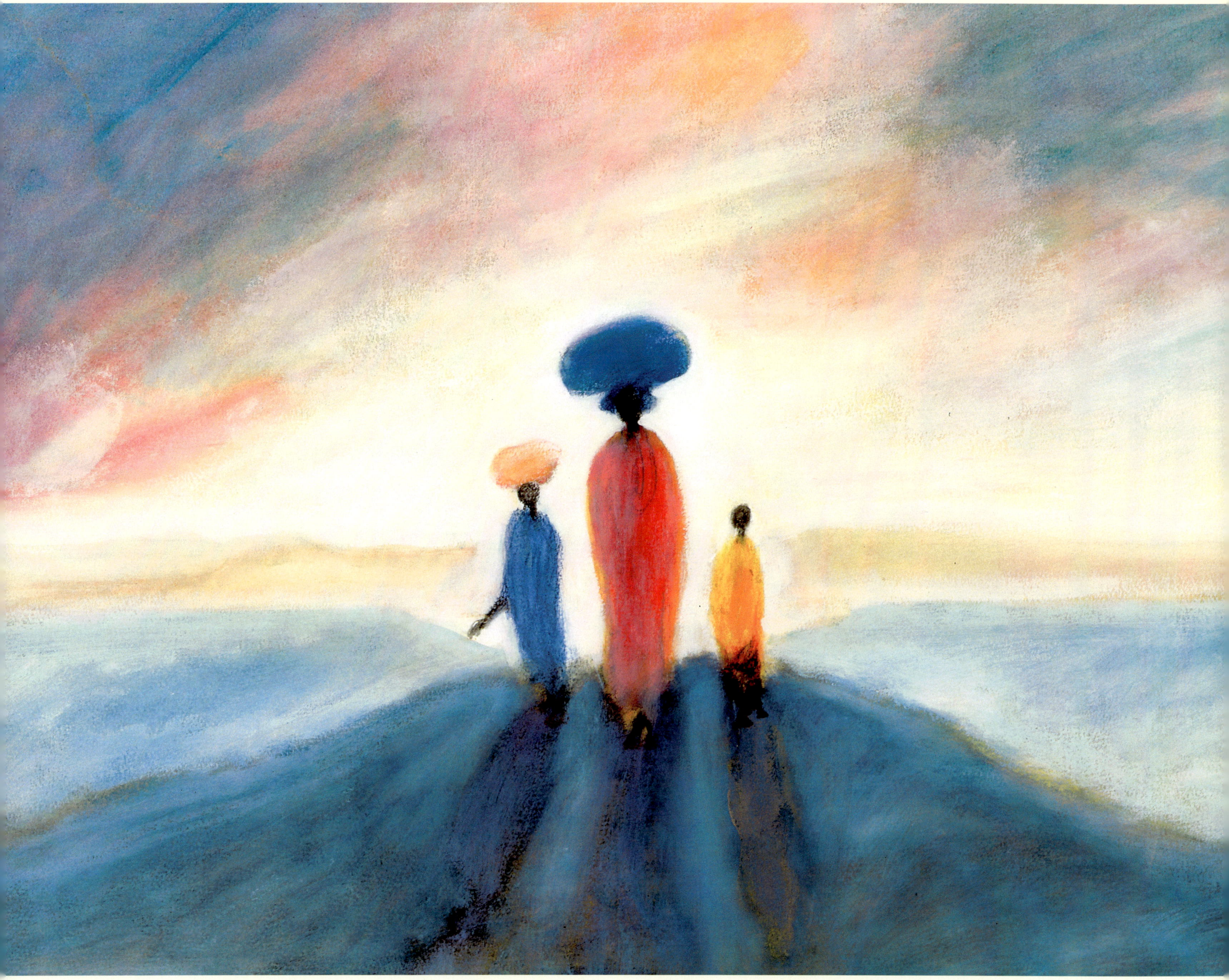

Coming Rain *- A trinity of figures face the oncoming clouds which bring welcome rain to feed the crops and fill the rivers. Water brings new life to barren lands.*
(Acrylic)

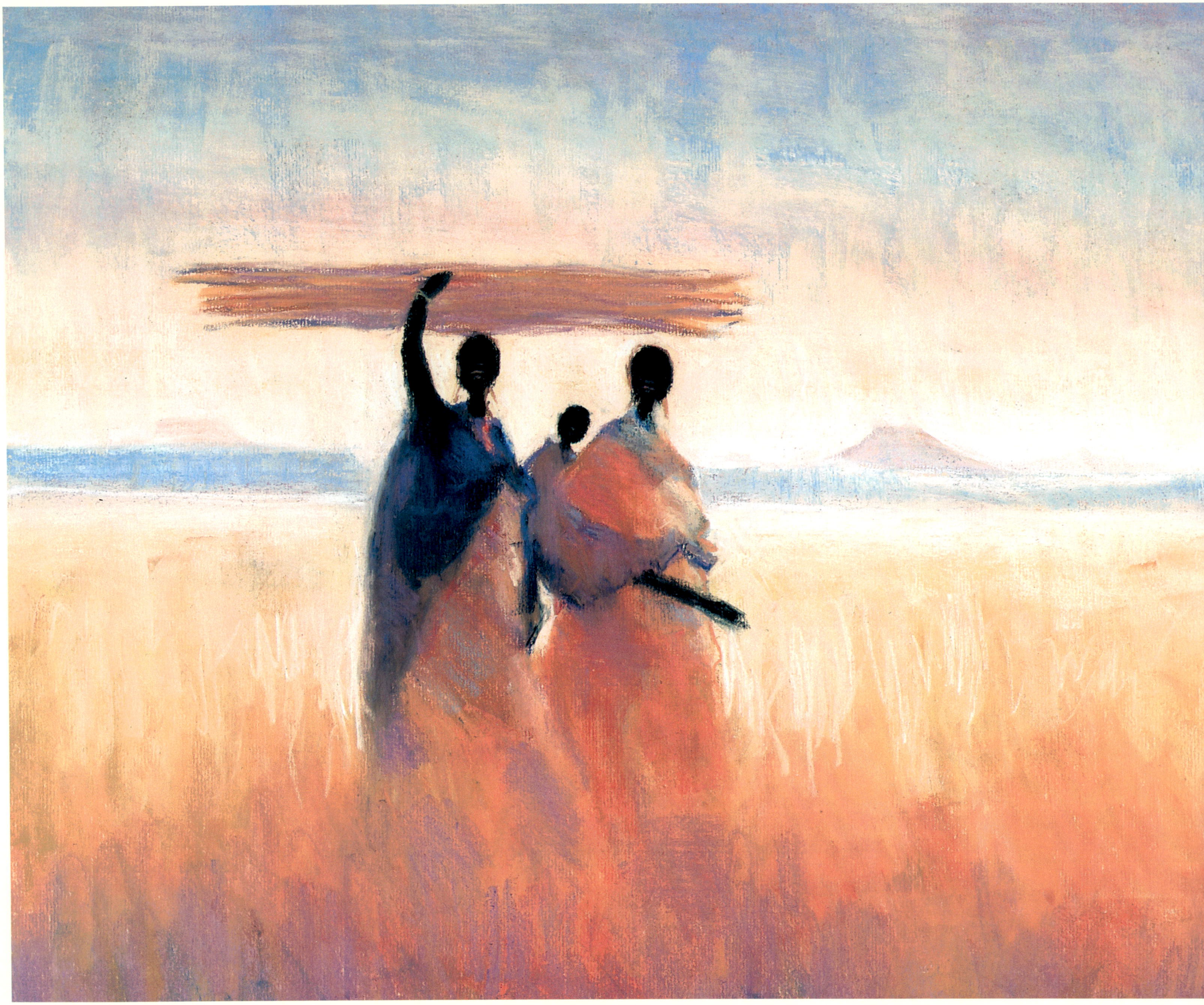

Returning Home - *The African woman lightens the burden of her chores by sharing it with others. When the firewood has been collected, she can return home to cook the evening meal for her family.*
(Pastel)

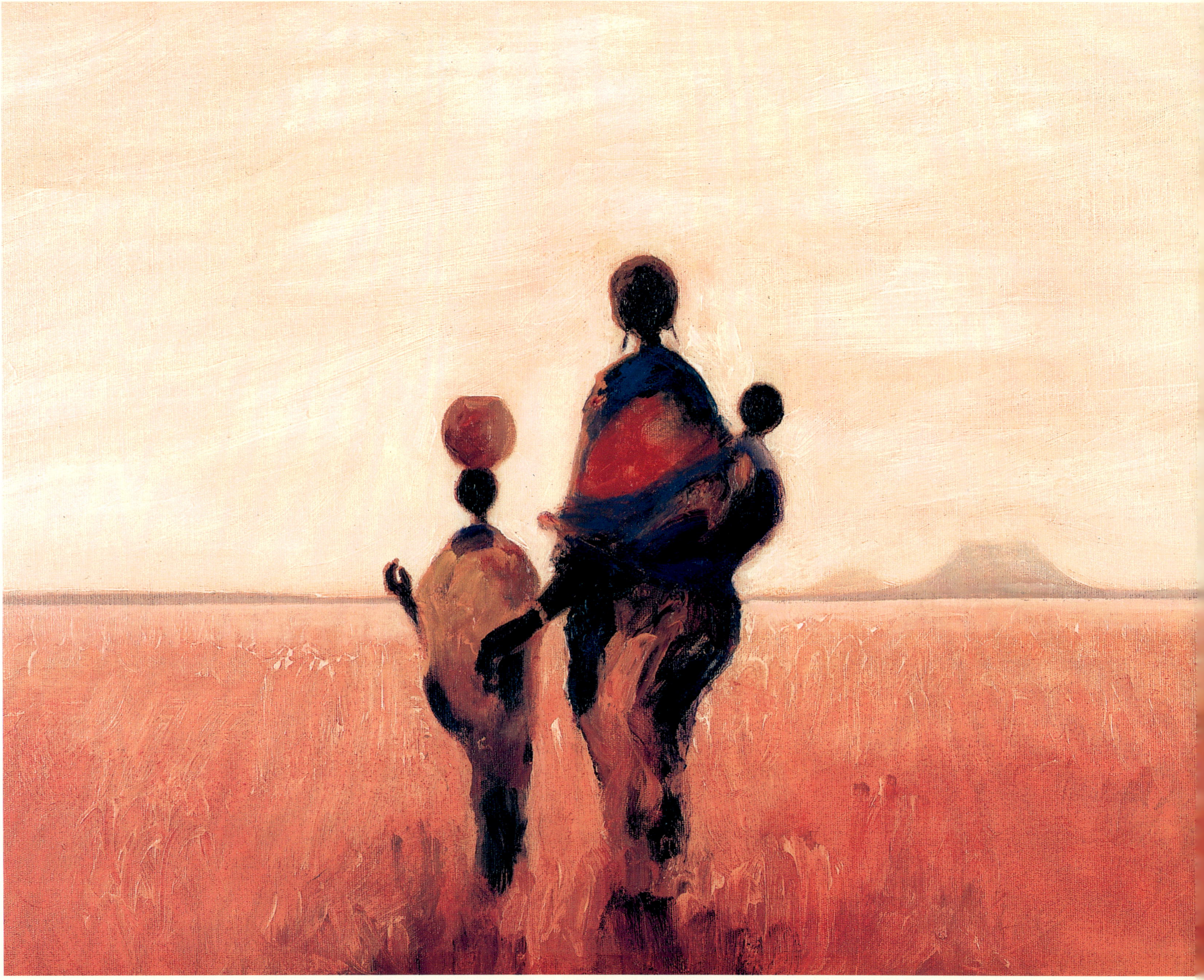

Mother and Children *- From an early age, the women and girls of Africa learn to move with grace and charm as they carry their belongings on their heads or infants on their backs.*
(Acrylic)

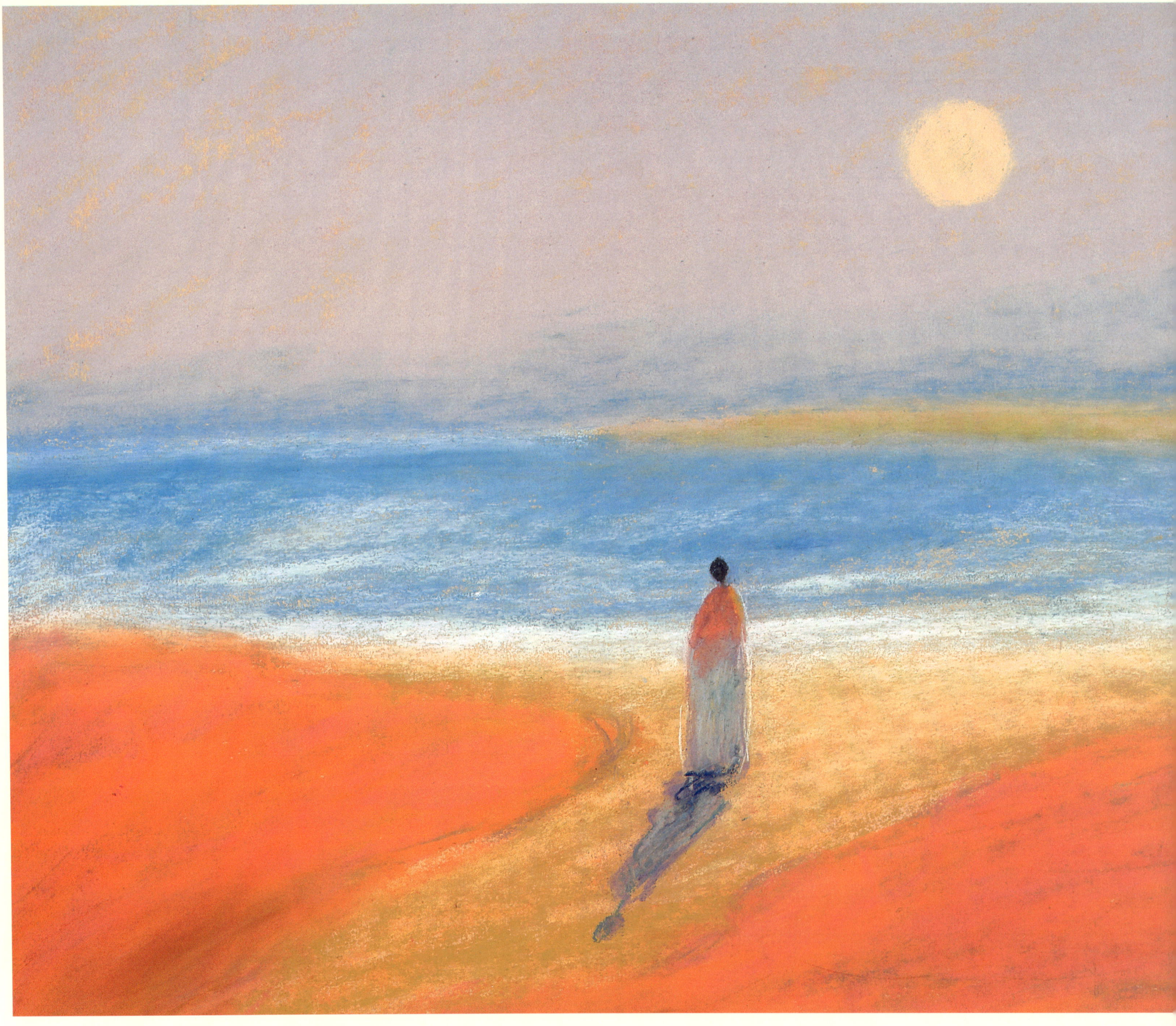

Serenity *- A women from the local village walks miles to fetch water from the river.*
(Pastel)

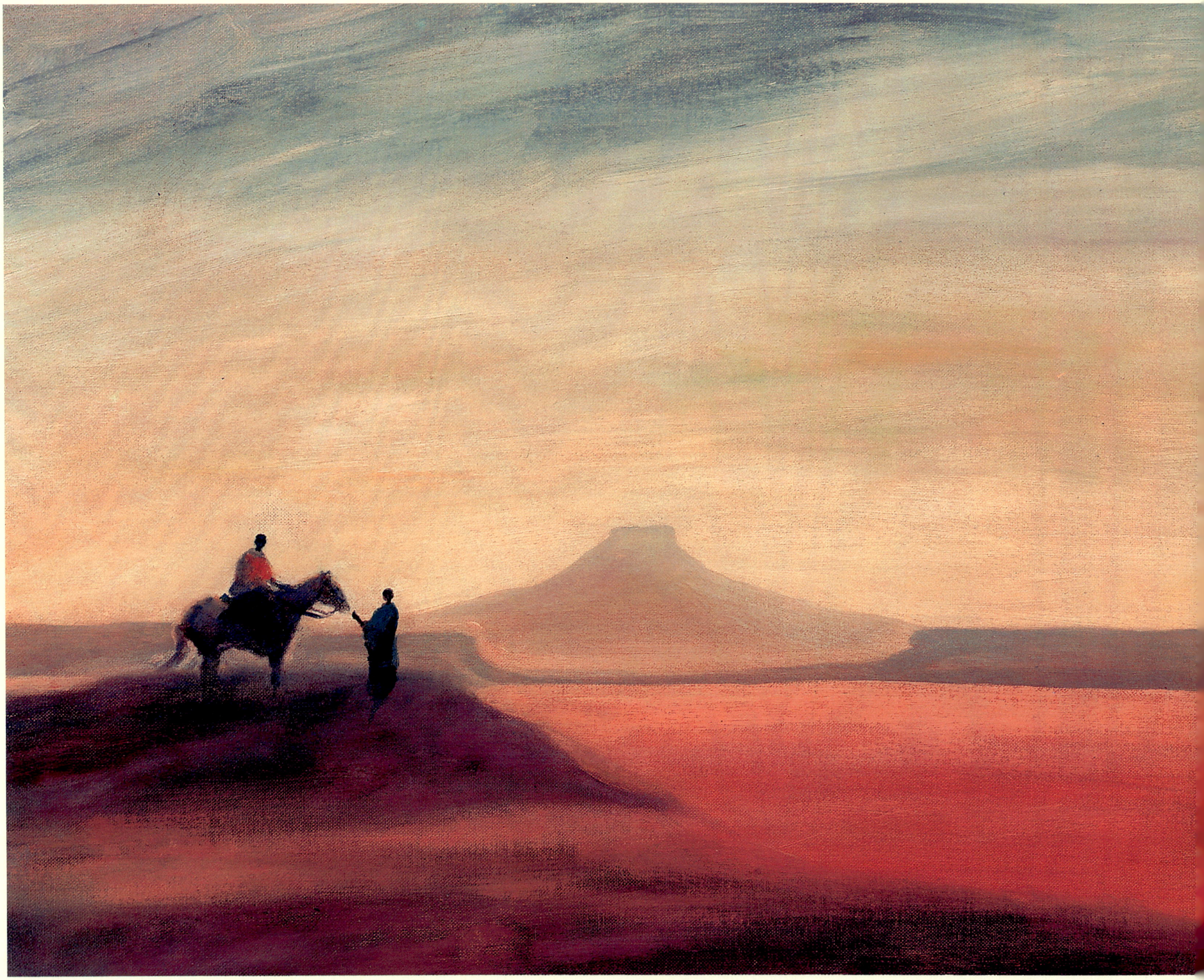

Dumela (the Greeting) **-** *A chance meeting in the remote mountains and passes of Lesotho is always celebrated. The polite conversation is begun with the word 'dumela' or good day.*
(Acrylic)

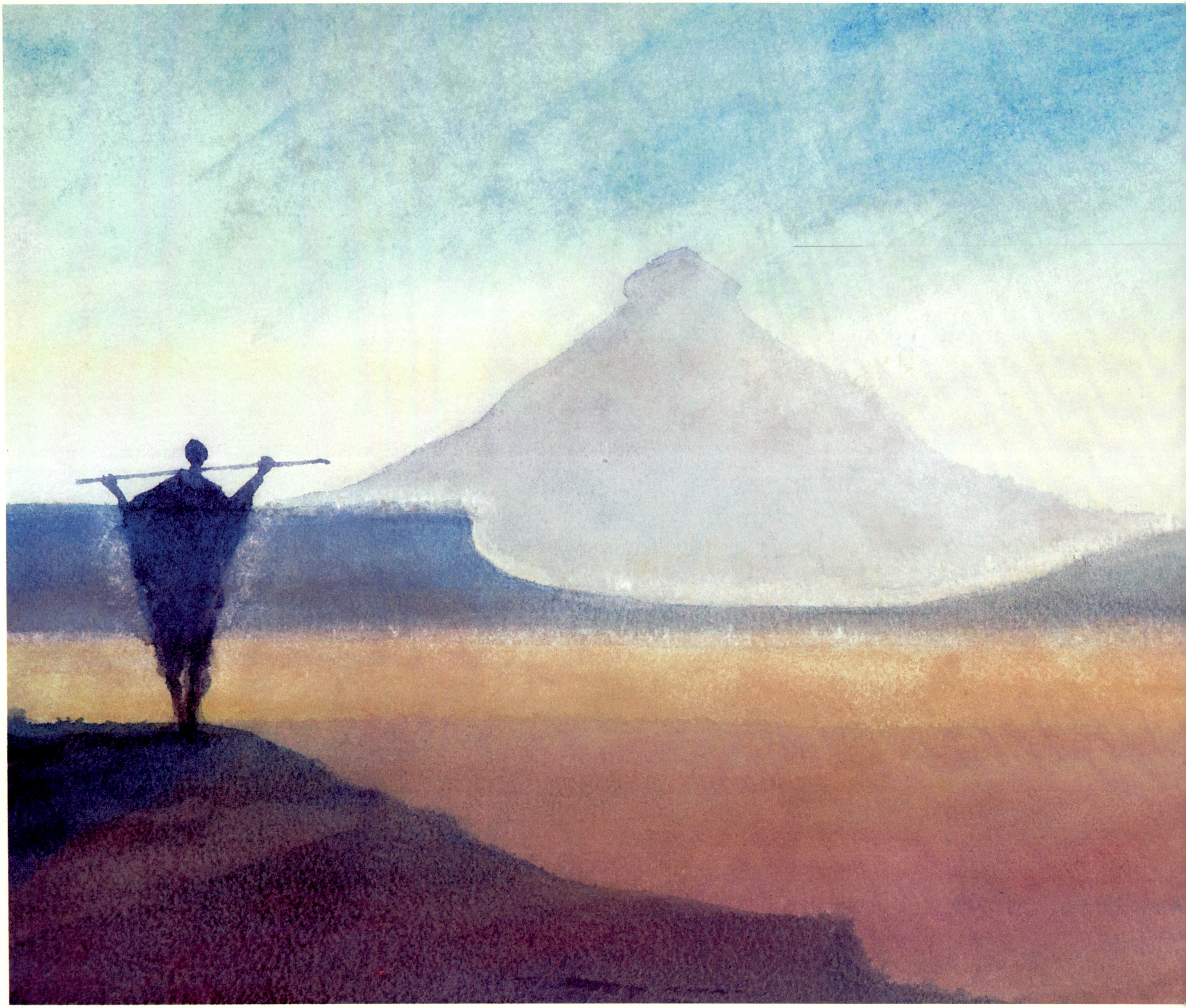

Early Morning - *The cold of the night passes with the rising sun. This herdboy is at one with the majesty of the new day, a noble figure in the Kingdom of Lesotho. (Watercolour)*

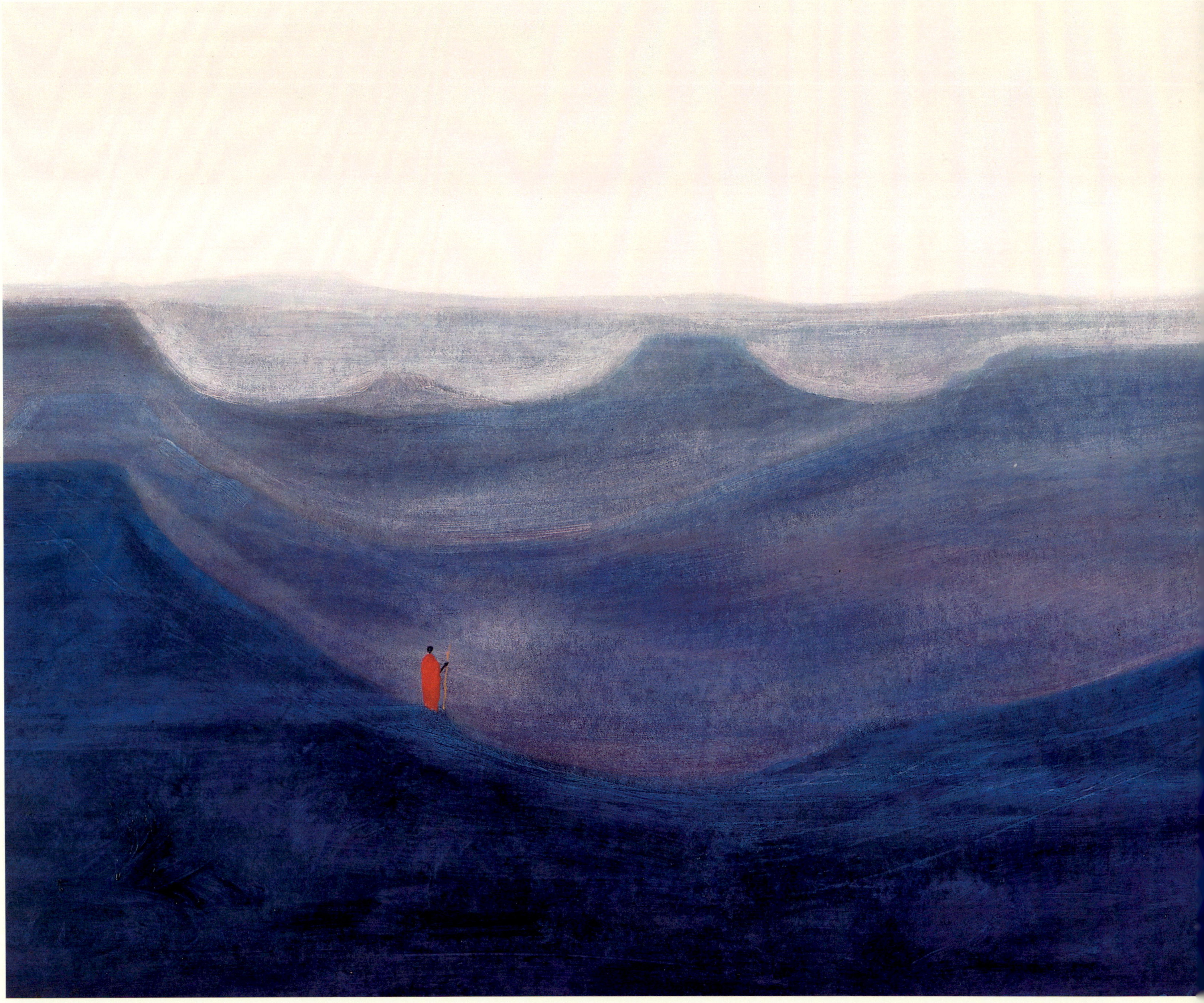

Blue Mountains - *Layer upon layer of receding mountains take on a blue hue in the light of dawn and dusk. In Lesotho they are called the Maluti Mountains, 'maluti' being the Sotho word for 'blue'.*
(Acrylic)

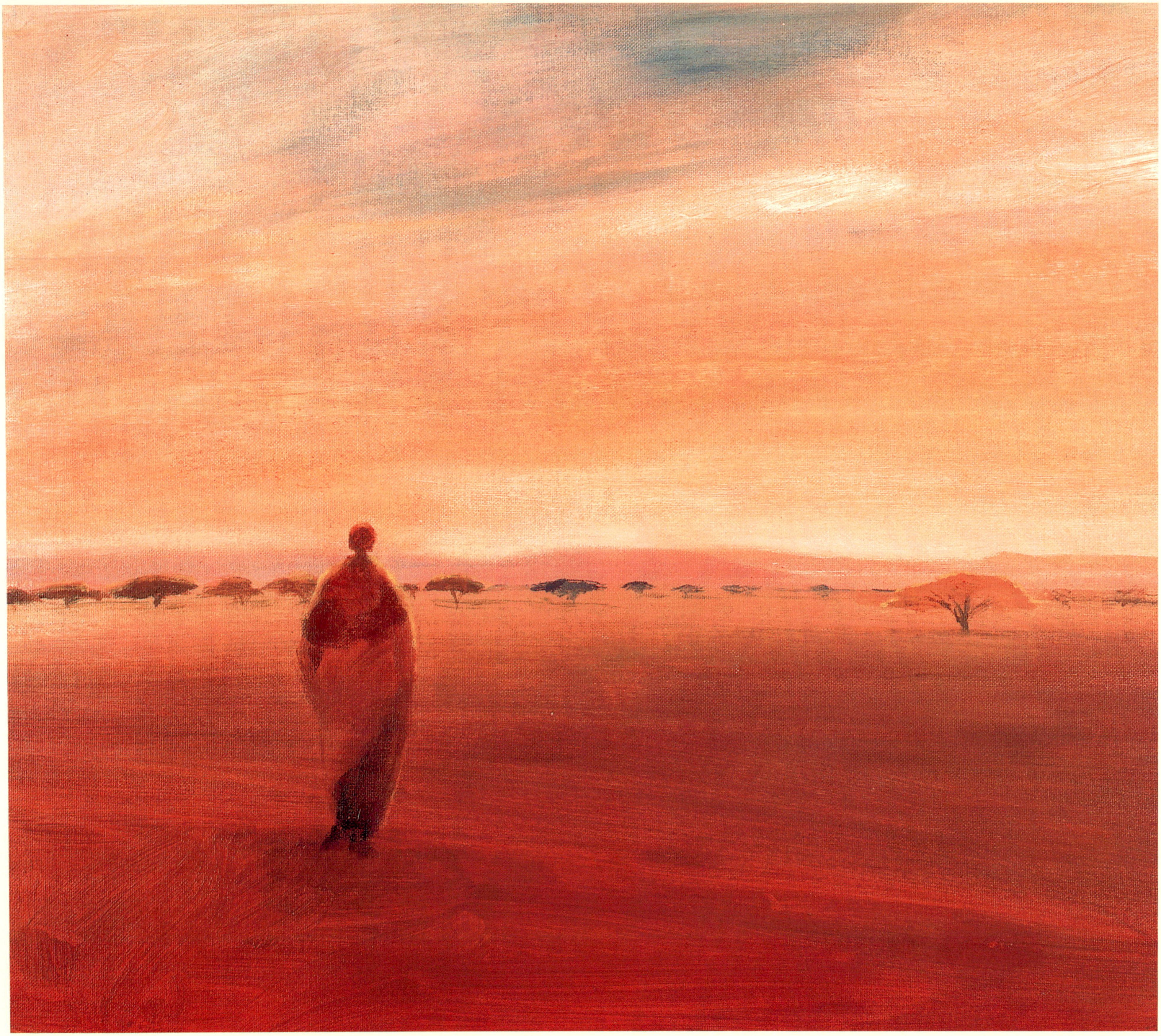

Early Evening - *Vast skies echo the heat of the scorching plains as the sun sets behind the distant horizon. Life, too, can seem an endless plain with few landmarks.*
(Acrylic)

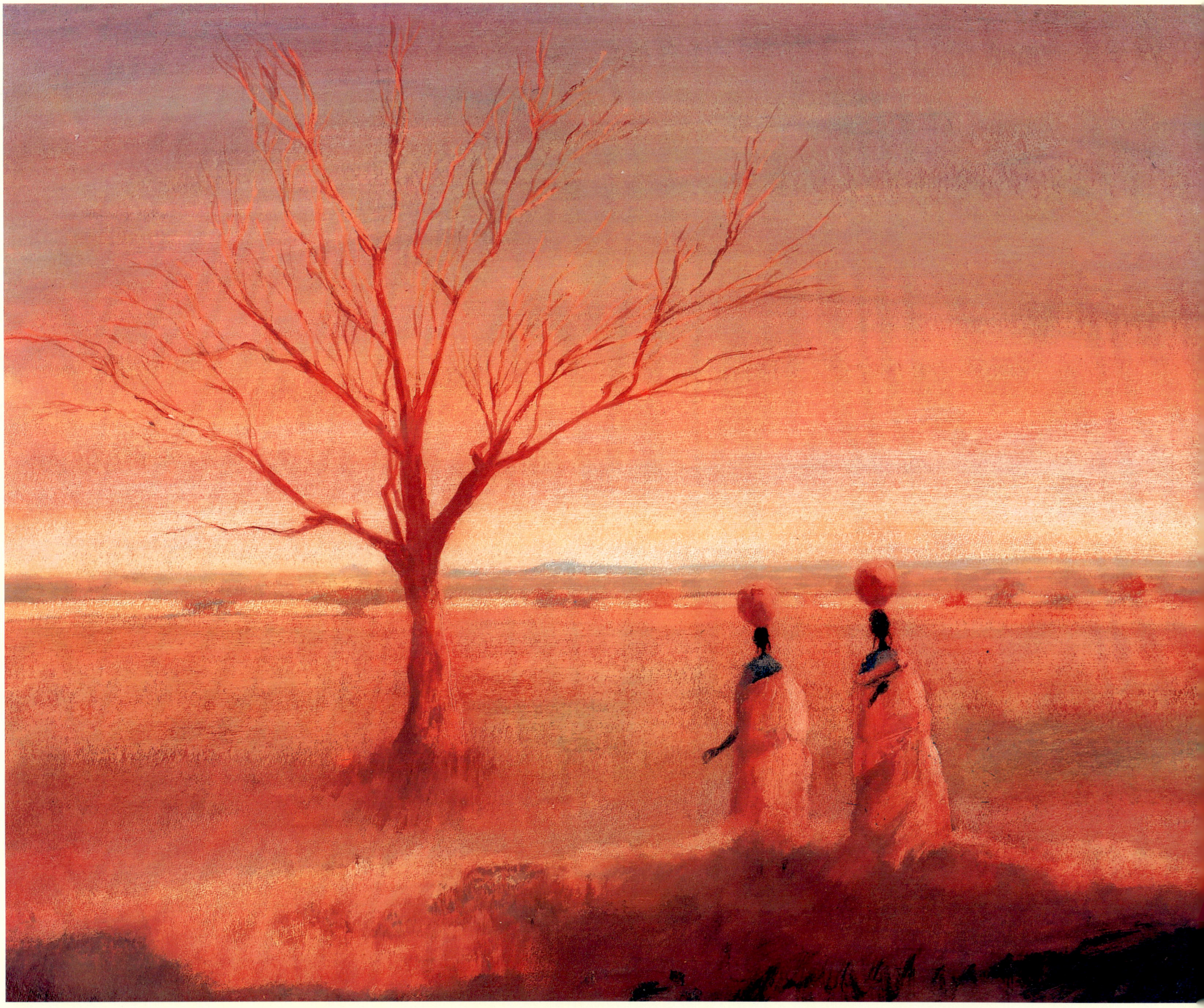

No Shade - *Shade for the travellers would be welcome, but this bare tree has been stripped of leaf and life by the harsh, unremitting African sun. Only the strength of the women goes on day by day.*
(Acrylic)

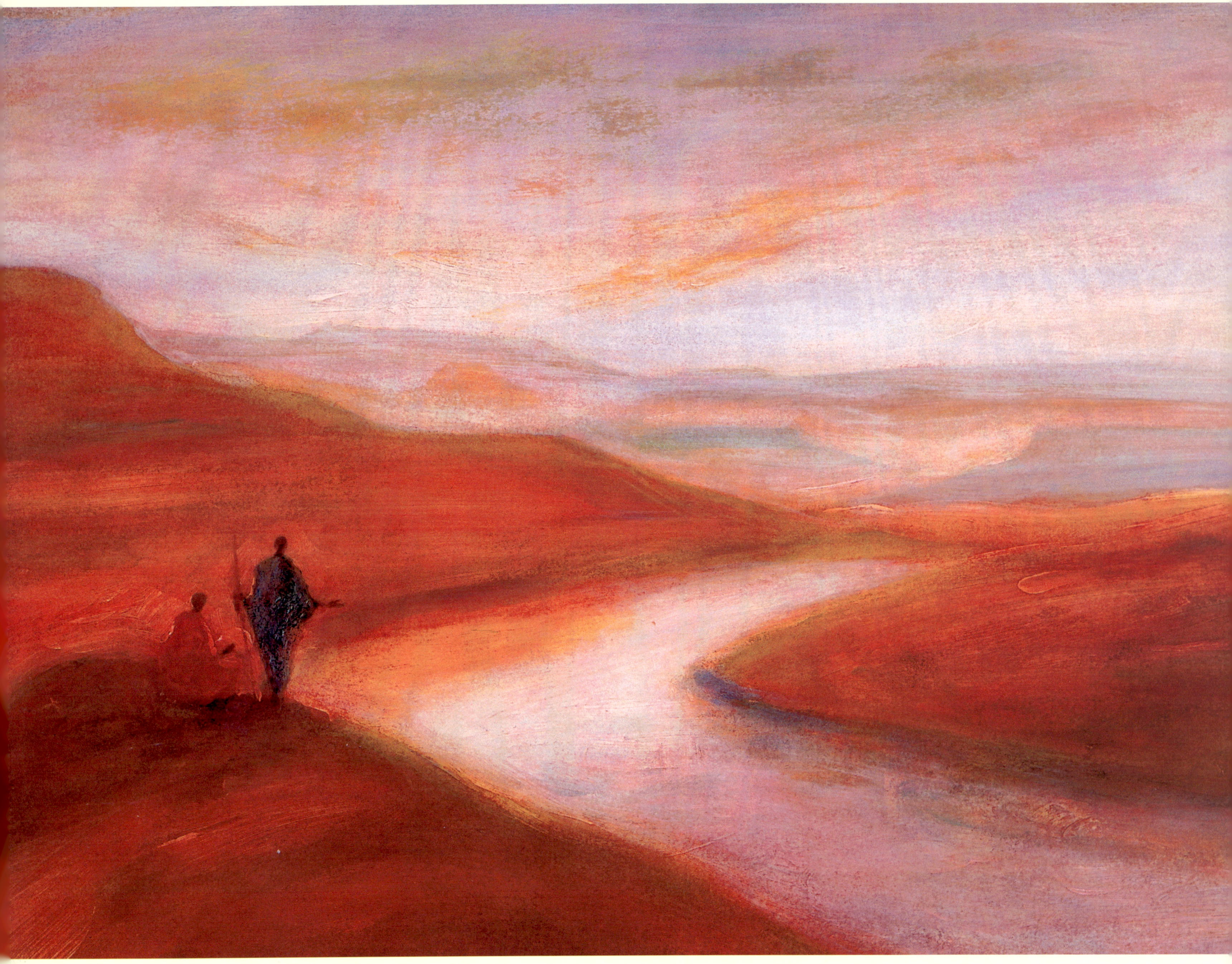

Above: ***The Caledon River*** *- The border between the independent Kingdom of Lesotho and the Republic of South Africa is the Caledon River. For many troubled years, this river represented the divide between freedom and oppression. (Acrylic)*
Opposite page: ***Expanse*** *- The glory and majesty of the Maluti mountains was deeply appreciated by Tony. To stand alone and free in such a vast space is to breath in power and strength from the very depths of the earth.(Acrylic)*

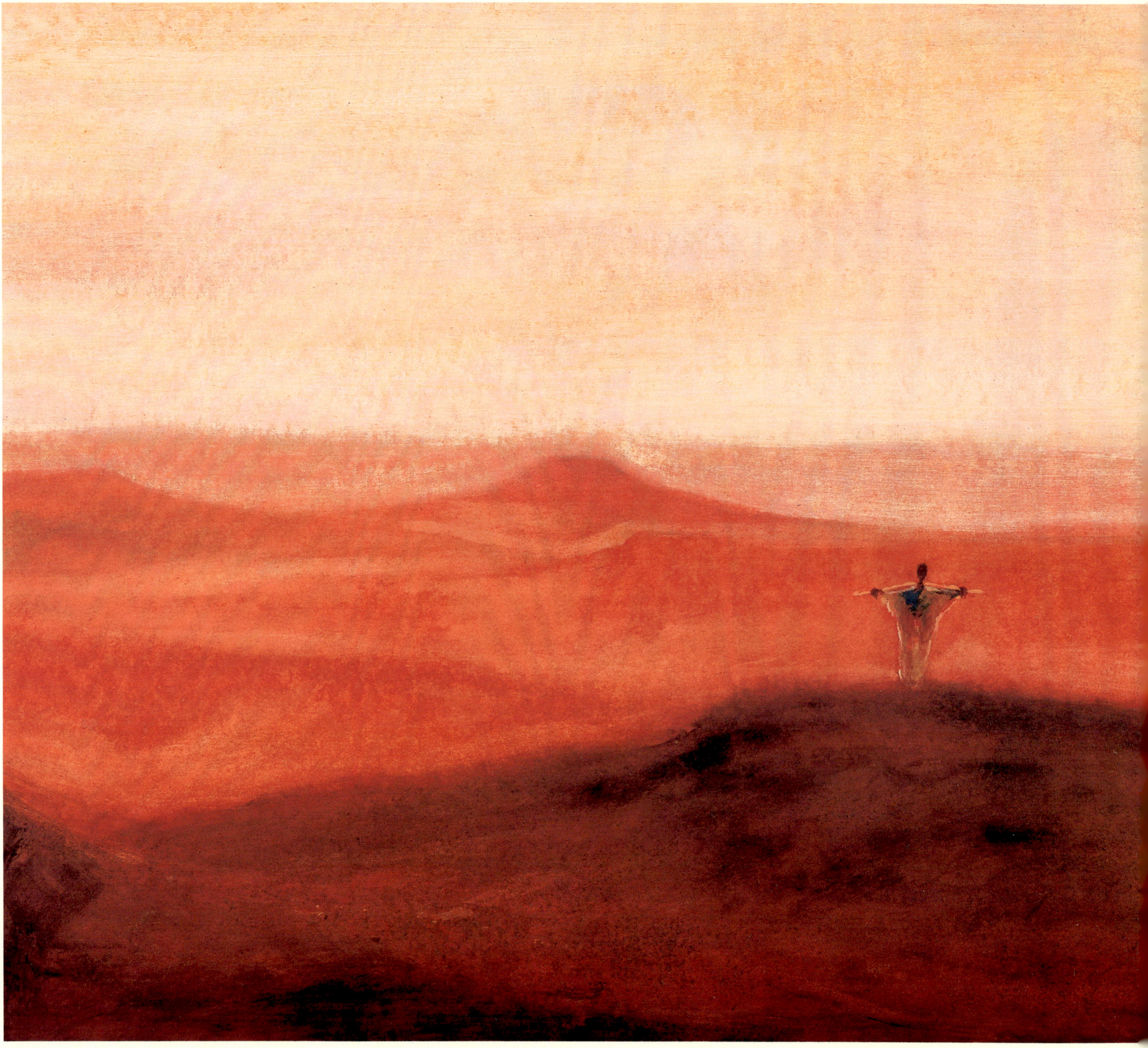

Credits

Producer: Dylan Hudson
African Connection
33 Fore street
St.Ives
Cornwall
England TR26 7RT
TEL & FAX: +44(0)1736 793147

Graphic Design: Louise Hillier Designs
1 Highfield Court
Wheal Kitty
St Agnes
Truro
Cornwall
England TR5 ORL
Tel & Fax: +44 (0)1872 553613
E-mail: loo@netmatters.co.uk

Editor: Bridget King
De Walden court
51 Meads road
Eastbourne
Sussex
England BN20 7QB
Tel & Fax: +44(0)1323 411483
e- mail: bking@hinge.mistral.co.uk

Printers: Focus on Print Ltd.
The N.C.T. Building
3 The Green Market
Penzance
Cornwall
England TR18 2SG
Tel & Fax:+44(0)1736 331188

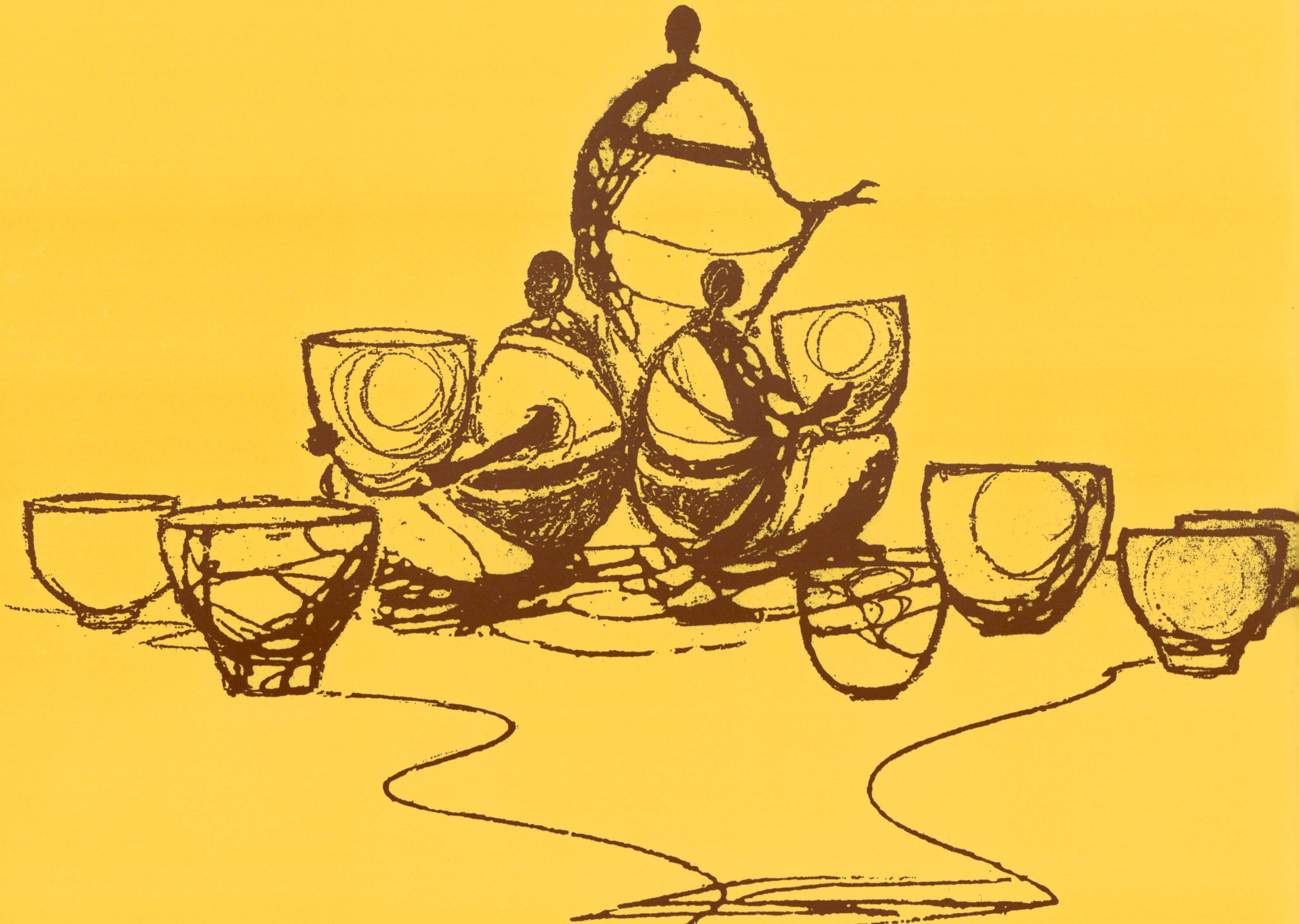